Galing-Galing

First Philippine cookbook for use in the United States

Food as prepared in Philippine Homes

National Book Store

QUAD ALPHA CENTRUM BLDG.
125 Pioneer St., Mandaluyong City

Published by

National
Book Store

Cover Design by
Cel Gulapa

3839

Printed by
Cacho Hermanos, Inc.
Pines Cor. Union Sts.,
Mandaluyong City

ISBN 971-08-2474-0

DEDICATION

To my grandchildren:
Rafael, Isabel and Ava
Franco, Ali and Arturo
Eduardo and Rodrigo
Toby, Bettina and Bolo
Gio, Billie and Joseph.

Foreword

If the title of this cookbook has a musical sound to it, let me give you a small anecdote that will explain it. While listening to Van Cliburn play, "Ang galing galing" could be heard from his fans. He then asked what the phrase meant and when told it meant very good, he exclaimed, "That Nora should be the name of your restaurant in New York." So to Van Cliburn, I say thank you for such an imaginative name for a cookbook.

In the first two editions, I included recipes that I liked to use in my home in the Philippines. It was to be a sort of handbook for the woman at home who wanted to use some tested recipes or one who needed to have her housemaid turned cook try her hand at the satisfying, challenging though sometimes tedious art called cooking. And with the comments I received from Filipinos, specially in the United States, I thought I would write one just for them. Many Filipinos abroad have told me that my first editions were their "bibles" in the kitchen.

Let me state right away that recipes in all cookbooks are guides and one's food sense must come into play in deciding the right amount of seasoning, cooking time and other modification needed for a dish. For food composition is not the same all over the world, and meats come from animals of all ages and breeds, so cooking time, flavorings and seasoning need to be modified to suit one's tastes.

I know. When we put up "Aux Iles Philippines" in Paris, we had to revise proportions for many recipes. Flour was not the same as that found in the Philippines. Vinegar did not have the same flavor nor the acidity as that of our native vinegar. Soy sauce was not exactly the same, neither was the "patis," a fish sauce called "nyok man" found in Vietnamese stores. Bagoong alamang was not to be found in exactly the same fashion we prepare it in our country, etc., etc.

Having lived in North and South America and now in Paris, I find that our food has not yet found its rightful place among the "Cuisines of the World." When I opened the doors of "Aux Iles Philippines," my Philippine restaurant in Paris, I did so with some misgivings.

True, I had invited friends to sample our cuisine for almost three months more or less daily (so my son reminds me and my maid did say, that my apartment in Paris was something of a restaurant) but it was not exactly the same as serving the public in general. But as patrons came to sample this strange new cuisine (for many Frenchmen think that in the Philippines we eat with chopsticks or that our 7,100 islands are somewhere in the Caribbeans) they did so out of curiosity. When they came back several times after that, told their friends about their "discovery", my confidence grew. My cup spilled over after only six months of operation, the prestigious "Le Monde" wrote a half page extolling the virtues of the new and fine cuisine they had discovered. The Guide Michelin 1974 gave us two forks and spoons similar to "Au Pied Cochon" of Les Halles (I never dared hope they would even mention us), the Guide Kleber put us in the same category as "Jun" a restaurant which cost at least ten times our little nook in the Latin Quarter and the Guide Auto Journal, a highly respected publication in France, included us among their "200 selected tables around Paris and Environs."

I am obviously proud of the recognition "Aux Iles Philippines" got. But more important, I have become aware of the innate flair Filipinos have for the good life. We do know how to live and eat well. Yes, you can point out to me the greasy fried foods we unfortunately sometimes find, but food badly prepared, carelessly handled exists in all cuisines. Our Filipino food prepared with skill, understanding and love can regale the most exacting gourmet.

When asked what is Philippine Cuisine? I can only inadequately say "It is the result of the Chinese, Spanish and Japanese (for we had them too for four years during the second world war) and American influences on our cuisine which we have created with the ingredients available in our country plus the ingenuity, the sensitive palates, the unique style and skill of the Filipino. Finally, our food is not really Chinese, not Spanish nor American, but FILIPINO.

What wealth we have in our cuisine. Where in the World would you find soy sauce and tomato sauce combined in a dish? Where would you find the use of rice washing, the heart of coconut palm (fresh) used in vegetable dishes or salads, where would you find the fruits, vegetables, tubers, shoots, tender leaves, many, and various leaves that go into our Philippine cuisine.

Where will you find the bount of fishes, shellfish and numerous produce of the sea in the 7,100 islands that make up our country? Where would you find the assortment of fruits, so varied and seasonal that we have practically different kinds of fruits to enjoy every month of the year. All these not to mention seafoods and meats which abound the year round.

There is much to be done, recipes to dig up, ingredients to rediscover, cooking afficionadas to seek out and ask to share their recipes so that Philippine Cuisine will be finally lodged in its rightful place among those that are the best in the world.

A word of advise. I have tried and tested these recipes with foods available in the Philippines. Each product may not have the same acidity, alkalinity sweetness (so many sugars in France are not as readily soluble as Philippine sugar for they come from sugar beets while ours come from sugar cane).

So, use your palate to guide you specially when you first try out a recipe. Make your own notes and modify the quantities suggested to suit your own tastes and those of your family. And as I often lecture my cooks in Au Bon Vivant, our French restaurants in Manila and Makati, it is easier to add salt to a dish than to reduce it. This is true of many ingredients. Adding too much of even a good thing can ruin a dish.

So for all the Filipinos abroad and other nationalities interested in food as served in Filipino homes — HAPPY COOKING AND "BON AP- PETIT!"

ACKNOWLEDGEMENT

This book is the culmination of some twenty years of work with food and people.

It began in Batangas, in 1944, when my late grandmother, Doña Cresenciana Reyes de Villanueva, taught me how to market, light a native stove, and cook rice. I remember one particular evening. She tore banana leaves into one inch strips and arranged them in a circle at the bottom of the clay pot. That portion, which is often encrusted with burnt rice, was now thick and wellprotected. She said: "When you are asked who taught you how to cook rice that way... you can say: my lola."

Then there was my mother Mrs. Encarnacion Guanzon Villanueva who taught me how to make my first Adobo, Sinigang, Escabeche, Cocido, Butterscotch Pie, Cream Puff and Pampango Frozen Fruit Salad.

As a student of the University of the Philippines in 1948, I acquired my first formal knowledge in foods, meal planning and cooking from Mrs. Matilde de la Paz Guzman.

In 1952, at the University of the Philippines Cafeteria, where I worked under the direction of Miss Adela Cruz Fernando, I learned more about Philippine cuisine and catering.

From 1955 to 1956, at Cornell University in Ithaca, New York, Dr. J. J. Wanderstock taught me about Meats, Fish and Poultry; Prof. Myrtle Ericson, friend and landlady, who handles food courses at the hotel school, shared and continues to share with me recipes she teaches her Cornell Hotel students. Then, there was Dr. Mary K. Bloetjes, head of Institution Management at the College of Home Economics who taught me portion control, recipe standardization, kitchen layout and management.

Back in the Philippines in 1957, as judge of cooking contests held by the Manila Gas Corporation over a period of three years, I discovered the different types of Philippine cuisine as influenced by the Spanish, Chinese, American and Japanese through all the years of foreign occupation. I also learned more about Filipino food preferences.

Turning to television as an exciting medium of demonstrating different types of foods — Chinese, Spanish, Filipino, and French — proved to be a double blessing. From my TV Show, "At Home with Nora" I was able to hoard quite a collection of dishes — those which can be prepared from inexpensive easily available ingredients as well as the more elaborate ones demonstrated by friends, restaurant owners, gourmets, and professional cooks.

As Director of the Manila Gas Cooking School, with the assistance of Home Economist Melania Almazan Trinidad and cooking "afficionadas" Perla Tablante Ampil, Virginia Domingo Perez, Katherine Lim and Lina Esteban Estella, I selected, modified, checked and kitchen-tested over 500 recipes for some 3,000 students who enrolled over the four years the school was in existence.

My first experience in putting out a cookbook was when the Carnation Philippines, Inc. asked me to kitchen-test recipes, compile and organize them for publication. The result was the Liberty Milk Cookbook which was widely circulated.

And so, here finally, is a compilation of all those years of work with food and people. Classified as Filipino, Chinese and European dishes, the recipes in this book are what I consider the tastiest, most practical, nutritious, reasonably priced and popular in the Philippines.

For a more comprehensive coverage, I have included here a few color photos the production of which I had the privilege to supervise. Those on pages 51 and 82 were used in the Asia Magazine, while the rest of the pictures were printed in the Liberty Milk Cookbook.

To all my elders, mentors, colleagues, and friends — especially to Mr. William T. Hiller of Carnation Philippines, Inc. who has always been interested in good and better food, to Mae Trinidad, Perla T. Ampil, Gregoria de Jesus and the men and women who work with me at Au Bon Vivant, I acknowledge my debt. Without them, this book would have remained what it was a long time ago — a distant possibility.

Nora Villanueva

NORA VILLANUEVA

Table of Contents

Hors d'oeuvres & Canapes

LONGANISANG SUMSUMAN

3 k. pork
1 hd. garlic about 10 cloves, pounded
1 onion, chopped
1 tsp. salt
½ tsp. salt peter (salitre)
1 tsp. Aji-no-moto

2 tbsps. sugar
1 tsp. whole black pepper (pounded fine)
1 c. soy sauce
¼ c. vinegar
2 pcs. bay leaf
½ tsp. oregano

Remove the skin from the pork. Cut into small cubes or grind coarsely. Mix salt, salt peter, Aji-no-moto, sugar and the freshly pounded pepper. Sprinkle the mixture over the pork cubes. Add the garlic and onion. Mix. Cover and set aside in the refrigerator. Heat soy sauce and vinegar. Add bay leaf and oregano. Continue cooking till mixture boils. Cool. Remove bay leaf and oregano. Pour the soy sauce mixture over the pork cubes. Keep in a clean, tightly covered glass container, and store in the refrigerator for at least 24 hours. Put in sausage casing and store in the refrigerator. To cook longanisa add just enough water to cover longanisa in a frying pan or a kawali. Cook over a low flame and allow water to evaporate. If pork is not tender add more hot water and continue cooking. After water has evaporated, fat from the pork will be rendered and the longanisa will cook in its own fat. Fry to desired stage and serve hot.

1

LUMPIA SHANGHAI

½ k. lean pork, finely ground
½ k. shrimps, chopped finely
¼ k. onions, chopped finely
¼ c. soy sauce

1 tsp. Aji-no-moto
½ tsp. salt
50 pcs. lumpia wrappers
Oil for deep-fat frying

Mix thoroughly all ingredients except lumpia wrapper and oil for frying. Take a heaping tablespoonful and roll in lumpia wrapper. Make a long roll about ¾ inch diameter. Cut to 2-inch pieces using very sharp knife. Deep fat fry. Serve with soy sauce and calamansi or Sweet Sour Sauce.*

Pinsec Frito

100 pcs. wanton wrappers (can be bought from Chinese noodle factory)

Place ½ tsp. Lumpia Shanghai filling into corner of wrapper, moisten edge of filling and twist wrapper to seal. Deep fat fry. Serve with Sweet Sour Sauce.*

* Recipe for Sweet Sour Sauce 1, on page 95.

PORK BALLS WITH GINGER

½ k. finely ground pork
1 c. coarsely chopped water
  chestnuts or sincamas
¼ c. finely chopped ginger

1 egg, lightly beaten
1 tsp. salt
Cornstarch for dusting
Cooking oil for deep frying

Mix lightly all the ingredients except the cornstarch and cooking oil. Shape the mixture into bite-sized balls and dust with cornstarch. Heat the cooking oil. Deep-fry the pork balls until they are cooked through. Serve hot on toothpicks.

EMPANADITAS

Empanada Crust:

4 c. bread flour	½ to ⅛ c. water
2 tsps. salt	1-2 c. cornstarch to prevent
¼ c. sugar	dough from sticking
¼ c. cooking oil	Oil for deep-fat frying
4 pcs. eggs	

Sift flour, salt and sugar. Set aside. In a large bowl, place eggs. water and cooking oil. Add dry ingredients and mix thoroughly. Knead until dough is smooth and satiny. Divide dough into two portions. Cover and let rest for at least one hour.

On a work table sprinkle cornstarch. Roll out dough to form a long strip keeping the width to about 10 inches. Roll out dough until it is paper thin. Wind rolled out dough onto an 14 to 20 inch stick (a piece of bamboo does very nicely). When the dough is about four or five inches in diameter (depending on the desired size of the empanada — a larger diameter for bigger empanadas) moisten end of dough and press on rolled dough to seal. Push out dough from oiled stick and cut to ½ inch thick slices (this will look like pinwheels). Roll out each piece till almost paper thin. Place filling in the center and moisten edge with water. Fold in half, thus forming a half-moon. Crimp edge or seal with fork tines. Fry in deep hot fat. Crust should be flaky. Drain out excess fat and serve.

Note: Pie crust dough may be used instead of above recipe for the empanada

Filling:

¼ c. cooking oil	and chopped
4 cloves garlic, pounded	½ c. beef or pork stock
2 onions, chopped	¼ c. raisins
2-3 potatoes, cut in cubes	2 tsps. soy sauce
½ k. lean pork, ground	1 tsp. salt
100 gms. ground beef	1 tsp. Aji-no-moto
10 pcs. green olives, seeded	Salt and pepper to taste

Heat cooking oil. Brown garlic lightly add chopped onions and cubed potatoes. Cover and allow to cook for one minute. Add ground pork and beef and the rest of the ingredients. Cover to allow meat and potatoes to cook. When meat is almost done, correct seasoning. Uncover pan and allow stock to evaporate. Drain out any excess liquid. Allow filling to cool. Use for empanada filling.

(This is a recipe I learned from a much loved grandaunt, Doña Luisa Villanueva).

CANAPES

Combine and make a spread with the following:

Egg-Onion Filling:

6 pcs. yolks, hard cooked eggs	1 tsp. salt
2 tbsps. mayonaise*	2 tsps. lemon or calamansi juice
2 tbsps. finely chopped onions	

Egg-Anchovy Filling:

6 pcs. yolks, hard cooked eggs	2 tbsps. anchovies, mashed
2 tbsps. mayonaise*	

Shrimps Filling:

½ c. chopped shrimps or crab meat marinated in lemon juice or French Dressing	2 tbsps. mayonaise*
	¼ tsp. salt
	1 tsp. mustard

Spiced Egg Filling:

6 pcs. hard cooked eggs, mashed	¼ c. sweet relish
¼ c. mayonaise*	1 can or ½ c. liver spread
	Dash of hot chili sauce

CHEESE DIPS

1 clove of garlic	2 tbsps. cream or undiluted
2 pkgs. cream cheese	Carnation Evaporated Milk

Rub bowl with the garlic. Mash the cream cheese and Carnation Evaporated Milk together. Add one (1) of the following; or, if you wish you may try a combination:

- 1 tbsp. finely chopped onions
- 1 tbsp. lemon juice or dayap juice with some grated rind
- ⅓ c. chopped crisp bacon
- 2 tsps. anchovy, mashed (wash anchovy with warm water. Add slice of lemon as garnishing.)
- ½ c. grated Queso de Bola and/or 2 tbsps. chopped Pimientos Morrones (canned red peppers).

Mix one or two of the above suggested ingredients to chilled cream-cheese mixture. Serve with dainty cuts of toast or crackers. I prefer to allow guests to make their own canapes as the toast or crackers get soft and soagy if prepared ahead of time. Simply prepare dips or filling and surround with buttered toast and crackers. If canapes are to be served at once, you may spread the cream mixture but butter the toast or crackers first. This helps prevent a soagy toast.

4   *Recipe for mayonaise page 141

BEEF TAPA

1 k. sirloin or other tender beef cuts preferably with fat	¼ c. white sugar
¼ c. brown sugar	1 tsp. salt peter (salitre)
	2 tbsps. salt
2 tsps. Aji-no-moto	

Slice beef thinly to desired size (preferably across the grain). In a bowl mix the rest of the ingredients and spread this on the meat. Allow beef to marinate for at least 24 hours in refrigerator. Fry in hot fat and serve.

Note: Use less sugar if desired.

DILIS FANS

½ k. fresh dilis, small ones are preferable

Batter:

1 c. all purpose flour	¼ tsp. pepper
1 c. cornstarch	1 tsp. Aji-no-moto
1½ tsp. baking powder	¾-1 c. water
1 tsp. salt	1 egg, well beaten
Cooking oil for frying	

Sift dry ingredients into a bowl. Blend in egg and water beating thoroughly to make a smooth batter. Set aside. Take 5 to 6 pieces of dilis and shape them into a fan, using the tail as a focal point. Dip in batter and fry in hot fat.

A better product is obtained by filleting the dilis, cutting it butterfly fashion, removing spine, dipping in the batter and frying. But it can be quite tedious.

5

SARDINE CANAPES

2 cans Spanish sardine in olive oil & tomato sauce
½ to 1 tsp. lemon juice
Tabasco sauce (amount depending on how hot
canapes desired)
Freshly ground black pepper
Salt to taste
Sliced bread and butter

Drain oil from cans of sardines and mash contents of the two cans of Spanish sardines. Moisten with lemon juice. Add a few drops of Tabasco sauce and freshly ground pepper. Add salt to taste. Set aside. Butter fancy cut pieces of bread and toast. Cool toast. Spread sardine mixture and bake to heat thru. Serve with lemon wedges.

CHICKEN LIVER WRAPPED IN BACON

½ k. chicken liver
1 lb. sliced bacon

6 c. boiling water
1 tsp. salt

2 c. cooking oil

Drop chicken liver in boiling water to which 1 tsp. salt has been added and allow to stay only until they are firm. Drain livers. Wrap each liver with a slice of bacon and secure with a cocktail pick. Fry in hot fat till bacon is crisp. Drop into collander lined with paper towel to absorb excess. Serve hot.

SHRIMP COCKTAIL SAUCE

1 c. tomato catsup
1 tbsp. finely chopped celery
1 tbsp. finely chopped onion
½ tsp. salt

2 tbsps. olive oil (optional)
2 tsps. lemon juice
1 to 2 tsps. horse radish
1 tsp. worcestershire sauce

3 drops hot chili sauce

Combine all ingredients in a wide-mouthed bottle and shake. Chill. Shake and mix thoroughly before serving. Note: Sauce may be used for oyster cocktail.

6

SIOPAO

Dough:

4½ c. all purpose flour
3 tsps. yeast
1½ c. lukewarm water

4 tbsps. sugar
½ c. pork lard or vegetable
shortening

Dissolve yeast in lukewarm water. When dissolved, add sugar and 2-½ c. flour to make a soft sponge. Beat thoroughly with a wooden spoon. Set aside to rise until double in bulk (about 30-40 minutes) add remaining flour and ¼ cup fat to sponge and mix well. Turn onto a slightly greased board using remaining ¼ c. fat (pork lard for greasing is preferable) and knead until smooth. Divide dough into 24 to 36 pieces depending on desired size. Form into balls. Flatten one ball of dough with the heel of the hand and put filling in the center. Gather the edges together and seal. Lay siopao on square piece of paper (sealed side under) and set aside to rise for 20 to 30 minutes.

Filling:

½ k. pork, cut into small pcs.
or ground coarsely
2 onions quartered
¼ c. soy sauce

½ c. water
2 tsps. sugar
½ tsp. Aji-no moto
6 hard cooked eggs, sliced
(optional)

Mix together soy sauce, water, sugar, salt, onions and pork. Cook over low fire until tender. Remove pork from sauce. Use to fill siopao. Add egg slices and steam for 30 minutes or until done. Serve left over sauce with siopao.

MARINATED PORK STRIPS

2 k. pork tenderloins
1½ c. soy sauce
3 tbsps. sugar
2 tbsps. minced onion

2 cloves garlic, minced
2 tsps. ground ginger
¼ tsp. sesame oil
2 tbsps. oil

Trim the fat from the tenderloins. Combine the remaining ingredients except the oil in a bowl. Marinate the pork in the mixture for three hours in the refrigerator, turning and basting frequently. Drain and reserve the marinade. Preheat oven to moderate (375° F.) temperature Transfer the pork to an oiled roasting pan and roast until tender, about forty-five minutes. Simmer the marinade for 10 minutes. Cut the pork into thin slices and serve on cocktail picks as an hors d'oeuvre with the marinade as sauce.

CHILI CHEESE LOG

Prepare 3 to 4 days ahead.
¾ lbs. grated cheddar cheese
1-3 oz. pkg. soft cream cheese
¼ tsp. salt

⅛ tsp. pepper
⅛ tsp. garlic salt
1½ tsps. Worcestershire sauce
Chili powder

Thoroughly combine cheeses, salt, pepper, garlic salt, worcestershire sauce. Shape into two thin logs. Sprinkle chili powder on waxed paper then roll each cheese log in the chili powder until thoroughly coated. Wrap in waxed paper and let ripen in the refrigerator for 3 to 4 days. Serve log on a board, surrounded with assorted crackers. Slice cheese log to serve.

Soups

CABBAGE ROLL SOUP

1 c. cooked chicken meat	2 eggs plus 1 egg white, scrambled then cut in long thin strips
½ c. cooked pork	
¾ c. apulid or water chestnut, chopped	4 slices cooked ham, in long thin strips
½ c. cooked ham, chopped	5 c. hot chicken broth
1 egg white	14 large cabbage leaves
1 tbsp. cornstarch	Salt and Aji-no-moto to taste
1½ tbsps. onion, chopped	

Chop chicken and pork meat to a paste. Blend in water chestnuts and ham. Add egg white and cornstarch, onion, salt and Aji-no-moto. Blend well. Parboil cabbage leaves. Remove the midrib. On each piece of cabbage leaf, spread about 2 tbsps. of mixture, arrange ham and fried egg at the center and roll. Steam for 15 minutes, then cut into 1″ pieces. Arrange compactly in a cup. Pour chicken stock. Serve seasoned with salt and Aji-no-moto.

PANCIT MOLO
Home Made Wanton Wrapper

2 c. all-purpose flour   2 eggs
2-4 tbsps. water

Make a well in flour, drop in eggs and 2 tbsps. water. Knead until dough is smooth and elastic. Roll out on floured board till paper thin. Cut into 3" x 3" squares. Set aside.

Can be bought ready made in chinese noodle factory.

Filling

¼ k. pork, ground
¼ c. chicken, cooked and
    chopped
1 egg

¼ tsp. pepper
⅓ c. singkamas or water
    chestnut, chopped finely
25 pcs. wanton wrapper

2 tbsps. spring onion,
    chopped

Broth

1 tbsp. cooking oil
6 cloves garlic, minced
½ onion, chopped
¼ c. shrimps, diced

1 tsp. Aji-no-moto
¼ tsp. pepper
Chopped spring onions for
    garnishing

6 c. chicken broth

Mix thoroughly ingredients for the filling. Wrap in wanton wrapper. Set aside. Saute garlic, onion and shrimps in hot oil. Pour in chicken broth and bring to a boil. Drop the stuffed wrapper into the broth. Season according to taste. Cover and let boil for 15 minutes. Serve hot garnished with chopped spring onions.

CHICKEN TINOLA

2 tbsps. cooking oil	10 cups rice water
4 cloves garlic, crushed	1 small green papaya, sliced
1 tsp. ginger, cut in strips	into serving pcs.
⅓ c. onion, chopped	1 cup sili leaves (pepper
1 stewing chicken weighing	leaves)
1 kilo, cut into serving pcs.	1 tsp. salt
1 tbsp. patis	1 tsp. Aji-no-moto

Fry the garlic in hot cooking oil until brown. Add the ginger and chopped onions. Cook until soft. Drop in pieces of chicken. Season with patis. Cover and let simmer for 5 minutes. Add the rice water, simmer until chicken is tender. Add the sliced papaya and cook until papaya is tender. Just before removing from the fire, season with salt and vetsin. Add the sili leaves. Serve hot. Serves 8.

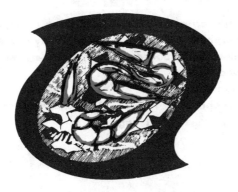

SINIGANG NA HIPON*

¼ c. onion, sliced	1 tsp. salt
¼ c. tomatoes, chopped	1 tsp. Aji-no-moto
10 pcs. camias**	2 c. kangkong leaves and
6 c. rice water	tender stalks (swamp
½ k. fresh shrimps, (med-sized)	cabbage)

Saute onion and tomatoes. Add the camias and cook until tender and mushy. Add the rice water. Let boil. When boiling, drop the shrimps. Season with salt and Aji-no-moto. Add kangkong and cook 2 minutes.

* *Shrimps may be substituted with fish such as lapu-lapu, apahap, talakitok. Kangkong, with vegetables such as mustasa (mustard leaves), sitaw, sigadillas.*

** *Lemon or calamansi or green "sampaloc" can be used to sour soup.*

HO TO TAY

Filling

½ cup singcamas or water chestnut, chopped
5 pcs. dried mushroom, soaked then chopped
½ c. cooked ham, chopped
¼ c. shrimps, chopped

¼ c. green onion, chopped
2 tbsps. soy sauce
1 tsp. Aji-no-moto
½ tsp. salt
¼ tsp. pepper
1 tbsp. cornstarch

1 egg

Broth

20 pcs. wanton wrapper*
8 c. chicken broth
20 large shrimps, peeled
1 chicken breast, sliced
¼ c. lean pork, sliced
1 tbsp. cornstarch
1 egg white

1 carrot, sliced
5 pcs. dried mushroom, soaked then sliced
1 bunch Baguio pechay or chinese cabbage, cut to serving pcs.
1 c. chicharo or pea pods

pepper and Aji-no-moto

Combine all ingredients for filling together. Wrap in wanton wrapper, set aside. Boil chicken broth. Drop shrimps one at a time. Coat chicken and pork with cornstarch and eggwhite. Add to broth. Simmer until done. Add the stuffed pinsec wrappers. Simmer 5 minutes. Put in mushrooms, vegetables and season with salt, Aji-no-moto and pepper. Cook until done. Ladle hot soup to individual soup bowls break an egg and serve.

* *Recipe of Wanton Wrapper, on page 10.*

CHAWAN-MUSHI CUSTARD SOUP

½ c. cooked chicken, diced finely

2 slices bamboo shoots, diced finely

¼ c. cooked peas

2 pcs. dried mushrooms, soaked and diced

¼ tsp. Ajinomoto

2 c. chicken stock

2 eggs, beaten

Place equal amounts of chicken, bamboo shoots, peas and mushrooms, in 4 individual pyrex cups. Set aside. Blend eggs, Aji-no-moto and cold chicken stock together. Pour beaten egg mixture into cups. Place cups in a pan and pour in about 2" of boiling water into the pan. Cover and steam 20 minutes over a low fire. Serve hot.

VARIATION: Chopped cooked shrimps may be used instead of chicken. Any green leafy vegetable may be substituted for the peas.

EGG AND MUSHROOM SOUP

5 pcs. dried mushrooms

2 eggs

3-4 c. chicken stock

½ tbsp. cooking oil

1½ tsps. soy sauce

1 tsp. salt

1 tsp. Aji-no-moto

Wash mushrooms, and soak in a cup of hot water. Set aside. Beat eggs, set aside. Boil chicken stock, add mushrooms with the water in which they were soaked. Boil 5 minutes. Season with soy sauce, salt and Aji-no-moto. Stir in the cooking oil and beaten eggs. Serve hot.

CLAM CHOWDER

3 c. clams (halaan) or about	4 tbsps. flour
¼ c. shelled	1½ c. Carnation Evaporated Milk
1½ c. potatoes, diced	1 tsp. salt
½ c. onion, chopped	⅛ tsp. ground pepper
⅓ c. bacon, cut into small pcs.	1 tsp. Aji-no-moto
4 tbsps. margarine or butter	1 c. clam broth

Wash, steam, clams (halaan). Set clam meat aside. Put diced potatoes, chopped onions and bacon in a saucepan. Add enough water to cover. Cook until potatoes are tender. Set aside. Meanwhile make thick sauce by melting 4 tbsps. margarine or butter in a saucepan. Add flour and blend well. Stir in Carnation Evaporated Milk and cook until thick. Combine potato mixture, white sauce, and clams. Thin mixture with clam broth. Season to taste.

RICE SOUP

¼ c. cooking oil	1 tbsp. rice wine
½ k. lean pork, diced	1 tbsp. sugar
¼ k. shrimps, diced	2 tsps. salt
5 pcs. sea cucumber, in strips	2 tsps. Aji-no-moto
8 c. chicken stock	3 tbsps. cornstarch dispersed
5 pcs. dried mushroom,	in ¼ c. water
soaked then cut in strips	½ tsp. sesame oil
3 stalks leeks, cut in ½" pcs.	1 large pc. burnt rice (tutong)
2 pcs. bamboo shoots, diced	or
¼ c. soy sauce	1 c. cooked rice, dried in the
	oven & fried*

Saute pork meat, shrimps and sea cucumber in hot oil. Add to stock and boil. Drop the mushrooms, leeks, bamboo shoots, soy sauce, rice wine, sugar, salt and Aji-no-moto. Thicken with cornstarch. Flavor with sesame oil. Fry burnt rice or dried cooked rice till it puffs. Serve soup topped with puffed rice.

* *Burnt rice (tutong) found at bottom of pot can be used. Dry it and fry.*

CORNED BEEF WITH ASPARAGUS SOUP

2 cloves garlic
1 onion, chopped
4 pcs. ripe tomatoes, chopped
⅔ c. or ½ can corned beef

4 c. broth or water
6 pcs. asparagus, cut into ½"
  pcs.
1½ tsps. salt
1 tsp. Aji-no-moto

Saute garlic, onions and tomatoes in oil. Add corned beef and broth. Simmer, and drop asparagus. Simmer 3 minutes more and season. Serve hot.

CREAM OF CHICKEN SOUP

¼ c. onion, finely chopped
2 tbsps. butter
3 tbsps. flour
1 tsp. salt

⅛ tsp. pepper
3 c. chicken broth
1 c. Carnation Evaporated Milk
½ c. cooked chicken, diced

Parsley, chopped

Saute onion in butter. Blend in flour, salt and pepper. Cook over low heat, stirring constantly, until smooth and bubbly. Stir in chicken and chicken broth. Bring to a boil. Boil 1 minute stirring occasionally. Remove from heat. Gradually stir in Carnation Evaporated Milk. Heat to a serving temperature. (Do not boil). Garnish with chopped parsley.

FRESH CORN SOUP

2 tbsps. cooking oil
2 cloves garlic, chopped
1 onion, chopped
100 gms. fresh shrimps,
  chopped

4 c. shrimp juice or water
1 c. young corn, grated
1 tsp. salt
1 tsp. Aji-no-moto
2 c. young pepper leaves

Saute garlic and onions in oil. Add shrimps and shrimp juice. Combine corn and simmer until tender. Season salt and Aji-no-moto. Add young pepper leaves 3 minutes before removing from fire.

LENTIL SOUP

1 pc. beef bone	¼ tsp. pepper
1 ham bone, cracked	3 sprigs parsley
1½ c. lentils	2 tbsps. butter
4 c. water	2 medium-sized onions, thinly
2 stalks celery, sliced	sliced
2 carrots, sliced	1 can frankfurters, cut
1 tsp. salt	diagonally

½ tsp. Aji-no-moto

In a deep pot or kettle, place the beef bone, ham bone, lentils and water. Cover and bring slowly to a boil. Remove scum. Add the celery, carrots, salt, Aji-no-moto, pepper and parsley. Simmer for an hour or until lentils are tender. Remove from heat, take out beef and ham bone. Force mixture into a coarse sieve and return to the pot. Set aside. Melt butter in a skillet. Add onions and frankfurters. Cook gently until onions are transparent. Add to soup and cook 10 minutes or until boiling. Serve hot.

SOPA DE ASPARAGUS CON PICADILLO DE GALLINA

chicken broth	6 pcs. asparagus, cut into 1"
salt to taste	pcs.
Aji-no-moto	1 chicken breast, (raw)
water from can of asparagus	chopped to a paste
3 tbsps. cornstarch, dispersed	2 eggwhites
in ⅓ cup water	2 tbsps. cooked ham, finely
	chopped

Boil bony part of chicken in 6 cups water until broth is tasty. Season with salt and Aji-no-moto. Add water from asparagus. Thicken stock with cornstarch. Add asparagus tips. Bring to a boil, then remove from fire. Mix chopped chicken breast and eggwhites. Add to hot stock while stirring briskly. Sprinkle with finely chopped ham. Serve immediately.

LOMO GUISADO

1 k beef tenderloin or round
   steak cut into 2" thin strips.
3 tbsp. cooking oil
5 segments garlic, macerated
2 onions chopped finely
   thin strips

4 big ripe tomatoes, chopped
¼ c soysauce
salt and pepper
4-6 c. beef stock or beef
   bouillion
½ tsp. Aji-no-moto

Heat fat in a saucepan. Saute garlic till brown. Add onion, ginger and tomatoes and cook over slow fire for 10 minutes. Add meat and soy sauce. Add beef stock ½ c at a time and simmer until meat is done and tender. Add just enough liquid to cover meat strips. Serve hot. Beef bouillon may be prepared with 1 c of water for every cube of beef bouillon.

CLAM SINUAM WITH MALUNGAY LEAVES
(8 servings)

1 ganta clams (tulya)
Rice water — 4 c.
1 tbsp. cooking oil
½ tbsp. garlic
½ c. onions

1 pc. ginger
3 tbsp. patis
1 c malungay leaves
¼ tsp. Aji-no-moto

Place the clams in a saucepan. Add 3 cups of rice water and cover. Boil for 5 minutes. Shuck clam and set aside. This amount will yield 2½ cups of clams. Saute the garlic in oil until light brown. Add the onions ginger and patis. Then add the clam, malungay leaves and 4 cups of clam juice. Cover and cook for 5 minutes. Serve hot.

18

SOUP SALAD OR GAZPACHO

1½ c. canned pork and beans
1 bouillon cube, dissolved in
1 c. water
1 clove garlic, mashed
2 tbsps. olive oil

1 pc. chorizo de bilbao or
   Spanish sausage, sliced
1 c. cucumber, diced
1 c. green pepper, diced
1 c. ripe tomatoes, diced

1 c. croutons

Puree pork and beans with bouillon water. Set aside. Brown the garlic in olive oil. Drop pieces of chorizo de bilbao. Add the puree of pork and beans. Cook until slightly thickened (about 20 minutes). Serve with the fresh vegetables and croutons.

SOPA DE MARISCOS

The head and fillet of
   lapu-lapu or any
   white-meat fish
3 cups water
1 onion, quartered
1 pc. leek, in ¼″ pcs.
4 pcs. alimasag (crabs)
30 pcs. halaan (clams)
¼ k. squid
¼ k. medium-sized shrimps
1 tbsp. parsley, chopped

¼ c. olive oil
1 c. onion, chopped
1 c. tomato sauce
   salt and pepper to taste
1 tsp. sugar
¼ c. olive oil
2 cloves garlic, crushed
1 French bread, in squares
2 tbsps. rice, uncooked
   salt and pepper to taste
2 hard cooked eggs, sliced

Boil fish head and fillet with water, onion and leeks. Evaporate until 2 cups of stock remains. Strain stock and set aside. Cut fish into chunks. Set aside. Boil crabs, pick meat, set aside. Boil clams, remove meat from shell. Reserve clam broth. Set aside. Clean squids and slice into ½" rings. Set aside. Clean and devein shrimps. Set aside. Saute onion and tomato sauce in olive oil. Simmer 1 minute and season with salt, pepper and sugar. Set aside. In a saucepan, heat olive oil and brown the garlic. Remove and fry bread. When crisp set aside. Add rice, squids and shrimps. Cook 1 minute. Pour in fish broth and let cook until rice, shrimps and squids are done. Put in the fish, clams, crabs and tomato sauce. Mix everything well and add more broth (clams) if necessary. Season with salt and pepper. Add croutons. Transfer to a serving casserole. Garnish with hard cooked eggs and parsley. Serve hot.

ONION SOUP

2 tbsps. butter or margarine
1 tsp. sugar
¼ tsp. prepared mustard
2 c. onions, sliced

4 c. hot water
3 pcs. bouillon cubes
4 slices French bread
1 c. grated cheese (Gruyere or Swiss)

Melt butter or margarine in a saucepan. Blend in sugar and mustard. Add onions, cook over low heat, stirring constantly for about 15 minutes or until tender but not brown. Pour in water and bring to boiling point. Drop in and dissolve the bouillon cubes. Simmer, uncovered about 15 minutes. Pour into individual heat-proof serving bowls. Top with slices of bread, and sprinkle with cheese. Broil 2-3 minutes, or until cheese melts to a golden brown.

SOPA DE AJO

5 segments garlic, crushed
¼ c. olive oil
2 slices bread, cut in cubes

6 c. chicken or beef broth
3 eggs, beaten
2 tsps. Aji-no-moto

salt to taste

In a saucepan, saute garlic in olive oil. In the same oil, fry bread. Set aside. Remove 2 tbsps. oil. Return the garlic in the saucepan and pour 6 cups broth. When it begins to boil, stir in beaten eggs. Season according to taste. Just before serving, drop in the fried bread or croutons.

Fish 'n' Sea Foods

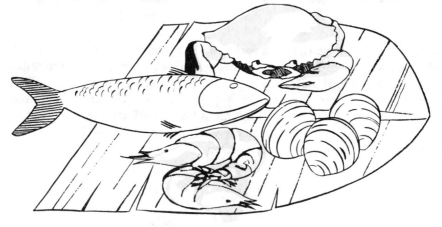

BANGUS EN TOCHO

1 med.-sized bangus about ½ kilo
¼ c. cooking oil for frying fish
1 cake tokua or beancurd, cut into ¾" x ½" pc.
1½ tsps. ginger, in strips
2 cloves garlic, chopped fine
1 med. onion, sliced

6 med.-sized tomatoes, chopped fine
2 tbsps. tajure
2 tbsps. tausi (salted black soy beans)
3 tbsps. vinegar
sugar to taste
3 tbsps. cooking oil for sauteing

½ tsp. Aji-no-moto

Clean fish, cut in pieces 1" thick. Salt and let stand 15 minutes. Drain. Fry in cooking oil until brown. Set aside. Fry tokua. Set aside. Saute garlic, onion, tomatoes and ginger. Add the tajure which has been dissolved in 1 cup of water, then the tausi, fried tokua, vinegar, Aji-no-moto and sugar to taste. Boil 5 minutes longer. Do not stir. Drop in fish and continue cooking 10 minutes more. Serve hot. Serves 6.

BANGUS SARDINES A LA ARSENIO LACSON*

A pressure cooker (size — about 4 quarts)
1 k. bangus (20 to 30 pcs. to a kilo is about the right size)
4 pcs. hot chili peppers (siling pasiti)
½ c. sweet mixed pickles

½ c. green olives
2 c. olive oil
½ c. soy sauce
¾ c. brandy
1 tsp. salt
1 tsp. Aji-no-moto
1 tsp. whole peppercorns
1 pc. bay leaf (laurel)

Clean bangus without removing scales. Place rack into the pressure cooker and arrange bangus in layers. Pour in the rest of the ingredients. Cover pressure cooker and allow mixture to boil until a steady stream of steam flows out of vent. Place pressure control on vent and allow to cook under pressure for one hour. Allow to cool before removing bangus from cooker. Bangus will be easier to handle. Entire bangus should be edible and is delicious as hors d'oeuvre or served with rice.

*Recipe given by Oscar Santos thru Rosie Valencia.

PESANG DALAG OR BACOCO

1 med.-sized dalag or bacoco
2 cloves garlic
1" pc. ginger, crushed
1 onion, quartered
2 tbsps. cooking oil
6 c. rice water

¼ tsp. peppercorn
1 small head cabbage
2 pcs. chayote
2 bunches pechay
2 stalks green onions
salt to taste

2 tbsps. patis or fish sauce

Clean then dip the fish in boiling water with 2 tbsps. vinegar. Remove dark skin with a knife (in case of dalag). Cut into serving pieces. Season with salt. Saute garlic, onion and ginger in hot cooking oil. Add the fish and pour in the rice water. Boil for 2 minutes. Add the peppercorn and the rest of the ingredients. Avoid overcooking the vegetables. Season to taste. Prepare the Misu-Tomato Sauce.

Misu-Tomato Sauce

1 tbsp. cooking oil
2 cloves garlic, crushed
1 small onion, chopped

4 tomatoes, chopped
2 tbsps. misu
salt to taste

Saute garlic in oil until brown. And the onions and tomatoes. Cook 3 minutes then add misu and mash mixture. Add stock from pesang dalag as needed. Cook 3 minutes more. Season with salt. Serve with Pesa.

PAKSIW NA ISDA
with Amargoso

1 Milkfish drawn but with scales intact.	1½ c salt water
1 med. size amargoso (ampalaya)	1 piece ginger, crushed
½-⅓ c. vinegar	Patis and salt to taste
	¼ tsp. Ajinomoto

Cover the fish with vinegar, salt water, and ginger. Bring to a boil; then add amargoso. Do not stir. Cook until amargoso is done. Serves 4.

KILAWING TALABA
(Pickled Oysters)

1 c shelled oysters, blanched
½ c vinegar
¼ c native onions, (sibuyas tagalog)
   peeled and chopped

3-5 peppercorns, crushed
1-2 tsp. salt

Combine all ingredients and let stand for about 2 hours. Serve cold.

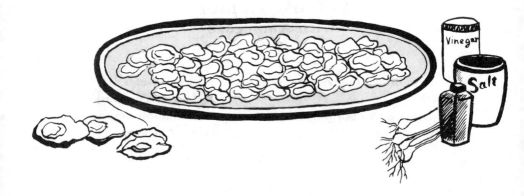

RELLENONG BANGUS

1 med.-sized bangus or
  milkfish (about 800 gms)
1 tbsp. soy sauce
1 tbsp. calamansi or lemon
  juice
⅛ tsp. pepper
  pinch of salt
¼ c. water
2 tbsps. cooking oil
2 cloves garlic, crushed
1 onion, finely chopped

⅓ c. tomatoes, finely chopped
1 tsp. salt
⅛ tsp. pepper
1 tbsp. butter or margarine
⅓ c. peas, drained
¼ c. raisins
¼ c. potatoes, diced finely
  then fried
2 eggs, beaten
½ c. flour
½ c. cooking oil

Clean fish. Pound to soften. Slit back to open and remove backbone. Scrape meat with a spoon or knife. Keep skin in 1 piece. Soak skin in mixture of calamansi juice, soy sauce and pepper. Set aside. Boil bangus flesh with pinch of salt and ¼ cup water, until color changes. Set aside. Drain. Pick bones. Saute garlic, onion and tomatoes in hot oil. Add fish and season. Cook 5 minutes. Remove from fire. Put in margarine, peas, raisin, fried potatoes, and eggs. Mix thoroughly. Stuff fish skin with mixture and sew opening. Dredge in flour and fry until brown. Arrange on a platter, garnish with kinchay, or Chinese celery, tomatoes, and slices of lemon.

ADOBONG PUSIT

½ k. fresh squids
½ head garlic, minced
⅓ c. native vinegar
¼ c. water
1 tsp. salt

½ c. squid broth
1 onion, chopped
6 tomatoes, chopped, (optional)
½ tsp. salt
1 tsp. Aji-no-moto

Boil squid in garlic, vinegar, water and salt. When tender, take out squid and remove membrane, eyes and stomach. Set ½ cup broth aside. Cut squid into 1″ pieces. Set aside. Saute garlic, onion and tomatoes in oil. Add squid's broth. Season with salt and Aji-no-moto.

LAING

½ kilo shrimps, chopped finely
2 small young coconuts,
   grated
1 onion, chopped
1 tsp. salt

10-15 pcs. wilted gabi leaves
1 c. thin coconut milk
1 c. thick coconut milk
2 pcs. siling labuyo or hot
   pepper

Combine shrimps, coconut and onion. Season with salt. Chop. Wrap by tablespoons in gabi leaves. Arrange in an earthenware pot and pour thin coconut milk over wrapped mixture. Cover and simmer over low flame, shaking pot once in a while to avoid burning. When almost done, add the thick coconut milk and sili. Continue cooking until sauce is thick.

SHRIMP REBOSADO

½ k. medium-sized shrimps

Marinade

⅓ c. native vinegar
10 peppercorn, crushed

4 cloves garlic, crushed
½ tsp. salt

Batter

¾ tsp. salt
1 tsp. baking powder
1 c. all-purpose flour
¼ c. water
¼ c. Carnation Evaporated Milk

¼ tsp. black pepper
1 tsp. Aji-no-moto
2 tbsps. atsuete or anato seeds
water (2 tbsps. water in 1
tbsp. atsuete)

1 egg, well beaten

Marinate shrimps in native vinegar, peppercorn, garlic, and salt. Cover. Place in cool place for 1-2 hours. Sift together salt, baking powder and flour. Set aside. Combine ¼ cup of water, ¼ cup of Carnation Evaporated Milk, black pepper, Aji-no-moto, atsuete water and eggs. Pour milk-egg-atsuete mixture into flour mixture gradually while stirring constantly. Beat until smooth. Drain shrimps. Dip marinated shrimps in batter one by one and deep-fat fry. Serve hot with catsup or Sweet Sour Sauce*. Serves 6.

* Recipe for Sweet Sour Sauce 1, on page 95.

CAMARRON CON PELLEJO

6 pcs. prawns
2 tbsps. white wine
¼ tsp. ginger juice
2 tsps. salt
⅛ tsp. pepper
¼ c. flour
4 tsps. worcestershire sauce

½ c. tomato catsup
¾ c. water
½ c. green pepper, diced
½ c. red pepper, diced
¼ c. spring onion, sliced ¼"
long
1 onion, sliced

2 tomatoes, diced

Cut prawns in diagonal 2" pieces. Season with white wine, ginger juice, salt and pepper. Dredge in flour. Let stand 20 minutes. Fry in hot cooking oil until crisp. Put prawns into a saucepan. Add worcestershire sauce, tomato catsup, water, green and red pepper, spring onion, sliced onion and tomatoes. Cover and simmer until done.

LAPU-LAPU WITH TAUSI

Fillet of Lapu lapu or any
white meat fish (500 gms)
½ c. yellow tausi (yellow
fermented soy beans)
1 tsp. fresh ginger, chopped
4 pcs. tokwa or soy bean curd,
in ½" cubes
½ c. taingang daga or black
wood ear, soaked in water

3 onions, sliced
3 tomatoes, sliced
½ c. all purpose flour
3 cloves garlic, crushed
2 tbsp. soy sauce
cooking oil for frying
2 tsps. cornstarch dispersed in
1 tbsp. water

Cut fish fillet into serving pieces. Roll in flour then fry till half done. Set aside. Fry tokwa. Set aside. Saute garlic, ginger, onions and tomatoes. Add ½ tausi, 1 cup water, taingang daga and cook for one minute. Drop in half fried fish and tokwa. Add the rest of the tausi and 2 tbsps. of soy sauce. Thicken with cornstarch dispersed in water. Cook until done.

SHRIMP ROLLS

1-2 tbsps. sugar
¼ c. soy sauce
2 tbsps. worcestershire sauce
1 tsp. salt
1 tsp. white wine
2 tbsps. calamansi or lemon
    juice

½ k. medium-sized shrimps
15 pcs. lumpia wrapper or egg
    roll
½ medium-sized carrot, in 2″
    pieces
1 bunch green onion, in 2″
    pieces

Prepare marinade by combining sugar, soy sauce, worcestershire sauce, white wine and calamansi or lemon juice. Shell shrimps, leaving tails. Devein. Wrap shrimps with 2-3 strips each of carrot and spring onion in lumpia wrapper. Roll. Seal with cornstarch paste. Deep fat fry. Serve hot.

SHRIMPS-SHANTUNG STYLE

¼ c. cooking oil
2 tsps. ginger, sliced
3 tbsps. tomato catsup
1 tbsp. white wine
½-1 tsp. sugar
¼-1 tsp. hot chili sauce

¼ tsp. salt
½ k. medium-sized shrimps, deveined
¼ c. shrimps juice
* To get shrimp juice, pound the heads of the shrimps and strain.

Heat cooking oil and fry ginger slices. Add the tomato catsup and allow to cook for a while. Measure in wine, sugar, hot chili sauce, and salt. Put in shrimps, toss till half done. Pour in shrimp juice, stir continuously while adding. Continue cooking until shrimps are just done. Garnish with wansuey. Serve hot.

RELLENONG HIPON

15 pcs. large shrimps (about 1 kilo)
¼ c. ground pork
⅓ c. cooked ham, chopped
3 tbsps. dried mushrooms, soaked then chopped

3 tbsps. spring onions, chopped
2 tbsps. carrots, chopped
1 egg
¼ tsp. salt
½ tsp. Aji-no-moto

¼ k. untosinsal or leaf lard

Peel shrimps leaving the tail intact. Slit the back and devein. Wash well and drain. Mix the ground pork, ham, mushrooms, spring onions, Carrots, egg, salt and Aji-no-moto. Lay the shrimps on a piece of untosinsal. Top with a teaspoonful of the stuffing and wrap with untosinsal. Dip in batter and deep fat fry. Serve hot with Sweet Sour Sauce*.

Batter

¼ c. flour
⅓ c. cornstarch

2 eggs, slightly beaten
2 tbsps. Carnation Evaporated Milk

½ tsp. salt

Combine flour and cornstarch. Blend in eggs and Carnation Evaporated Milk. Beat until smooth. Season with salt.

* Recipe for Sweet Sour Sauce 1, on page 95.

FILLET OF SOLE WITH LEMON BUTTER SAUCE

4 pcs. fillet of sole
½ tsp. salt
¼ tsp. pepper

1 tsp. lemon juice
¼ c. flour
¼ c. butter

Lemon Butter Sauce

½ c. butter, melted
1 tbsp. lemon juice
1 tbsp. parsley, chopped

Combine ingredients for sauce. Set aside, keep hot. Season fillet with salt, pepper, and lemon juice. Dredge lightly in flour. Brown gently in butter. Arrange in a platter and pour Lemon Butter Sauce. Serve hot.

SHRIMP TOAST

½ k. shrimps, minced
1 tsp. ginger juice
1 tsp. white wine
1 tsp. salt
1 egg white
½ tsp. MSG

1 tsp. cornstarch
6 slices bread, trimmed and
    quartered
2 tbsps. chopped ham
2 tbsps. chopped parsley
    cooking oil for deep frying

Mix first 7 ingredients together. Spoon a heaping tbsp. of shrimp mixture on each square of bread. Sprinkle with chopped ham and parsley. Heat cooking oil and deep fat fry bread squares, first with shrimp mixture down, then with bread side down. Fry until bread turns golden. Remove from oil and serve hot.

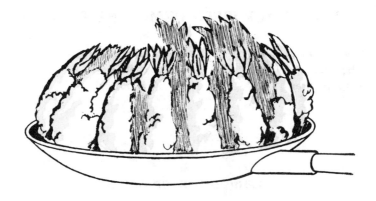

TEMPURA

½ k. fresh shrimps
1 c. all-purpose flour, sifted

1 c. water
1 egg, slightly beaten

¼ tsp. salt

Shell shrimps, slit the back and open butterfly fashion.   Devein and wash thoroughly.   Dry.   Set aside in a cool place.   In a bowl prepare the batter by combining water, egg, flour and salt   Stir 5 times.   Mixture should be lumpy.   Dip shrimps in the batter and deep fat fry.   Serve hot with Tempura Sauce.

Tempura Sauce

½ c. hot water
1 pc. bouillon cube
2 tbsps. soy sauce

1 tbsp. sugar
½ tsp. Aji-no-moto
1 tsp. ginger, grated

2 tbsps. radish, grated

Combine all ingredients together and serve with tempura.

DININGDING
(4 servings)

Daing (dalag about 100-150 gms.)
¼ k. chayote sliced
2 calabasa
2 large tomatoes cut into
    quarters

1 c. sitao cut to 1½" lengths
1 c malungay leaves
1½-2 tbsp. bagoong
1 c. Rice Washing
¼ tsp. Aji-no-moto

Broil the daing and cut into quarters. Mix all the above ingredients except the leaves. Cover and cook for about 10 minutes. Add leafy vegetables and cook for about 5-10 minutes more. Correct seasoning and serve hot.

DULONG OMELET
(4 servings)

3 tbsp. cooking oil
3 cloves garlic, macerated
1 med. onion, sliced
2 med. tomatoes, chopped

Salt and pepper to taste
1 c. Dulong
3 eggs
2-4 tbsps. oil for frying omelet

Saute the garlic in 3 tbsps. of oil until golden brown. Add the onions and the tomatoes. Season with salt and pepper and cook for 5 minutes. Add the dulong and stir to prevent scorching. Set aside. Beat the egg white until stiff. Add yolks and enough salt to taste. Pour about ½ c. beaten eggs into a hot, greased frying pan. Spread ⅓ of cooked dulong mixture and fold egg over. Turn over. Repeat. Makes 3 omelets.

CRAB FILLED AVOCADO

4 Avocados, cut in half, chill
  and set aside
Filling:
4 cups sour cream
2 tsp. Curry Powder
3 pcs. green onions, chopped
  finely

⅛ Teaspoon black pepper
½ teaspoon salt
½ cup shredded coconut (reserve
  ½ c for topping)
1½ Crab Meat

Mix all ingredients for filling. Chill mixture at least 3 hours before serving. Fill avocado halves with mixture and top with shredded coconut. Serve well chilled.

GUINATAANG HIPON OR CRAB

1 k. fresh shrimps or live crabs
3 cloves of garlic
1 onion, chopped
1½ coco cream of 2 coconuts
1 pc. ginger, size of a thumb
  and pounded

1 pc. dilao, pounded
1-3 pieces hot pepper (according
  to taste)
½ tsp. salt
⅓ c. green onion, cut 1 cm. long

Shell shrimps, devein, place in a saucepan. Add the thin coconut milk, ginger and dilao. Let boil until shrimps turn red. Add coco cream, hot pepper and salt. Just before serving, add green onions.

FISH WITH BREAD SAUCE

8 slices loaf bread, trimmed
1 c. hot water
Fish heads and bones
2 c. water
1 tsp. salt

½ lb. butter
2 egg yolks
2 tsps. parsley, chopped
4 fillet of any white meat fish
2 tsps. salt

¼ c. white wine

Soak bread in hot water.   Cool, then squeeze out excess liquid.   Set aside. In a saucepan, combine the fish heads and bones, water and salt. Boil until only ½ cup of stock remains.   Strain and set aside.   Cream butter.   Blend in yolks, parsley and bread.   Set aside.   Lay fish fillet on a greased baking dish.   Sprinkle with salt.   Pour in white wine and stock.   Top with bread mixture.   Bake at 375°F. for 20 minutes or until done.   Serve hot.

SHRIMPS WITH SWEET PEAS

½ k. medium-sized fresh
   shrimps
½ c. cooking oil
6 pcs. dried mushrooms,
   soaked then diced
½ c. bamboo shoots, diced

2 tsps. soy sauce
1 tsp. Aji-no-moto
1 tbsp. oyster sauce
1 tbsp. rice wine
1 c. cooked sweet peas
1 tbsp. cornstarch dispersed in

2 tbsps. water

Shell and devein shrimps.   Rinse thoroughly, dry on a towel.   Heat ¼ cup oil in pan.   Saute mushrooms and bamboo shoots.   Season with soy sauce, Aji-no-moto, oyster sauce and rice wine.   Stir in shrimps and sweet peas.   Cook 2 minutes.   Thicken with cornstarch.   Serve immediately.

FISH STICKS — ITALIAN STYLE

¼ c. all-purpose flour
1 tsp. salt
¼ tsp. pepper
½ k. fish fillet of any white
    meat fish, in sticks 1″ x 3″

1 egg, slightly beaten
1 tsp. Carnation Evaporated Milk
1 tsp. parsley, chopped
⅓ c. grated cheese
½ c. olive oil or cooking oil

Measure flour, salt and pepper in a paper or plastic bag. Put in fish sticks, 2-3 pieces at a time and shake. Combine eggs, Carnation Evaporated Milk and parsley. Dip floured fish sticks into this mixture, then roll in grated cheese. Brown in olive oil. Serve hot.

FISH WITH CARNATION SAUCE

1 medium-sized bangus,
    about 900 gms.
3 big tomatoes, chopped
½ c. spring onions, chopped
1 tsp. salt

1 c. Carnation Evaporated Milk
1 tbsp. calamansi juice or 1
    tbsp. vinegar
margarine or shortening
banana leaf

Clean fish. Do not remove scales. Slit at the back, remove intestines and gills. Set aside. Chop tomatoes and green onions. Put them in a bowl and pour the Carnation Evaporated Milk. Season with salt. Add calamansi juice or vinegar and strain the mixture. Set milk aside to be used for sauce. Stuff the fish with the onion-tomato mixture. Dot with 1 tbsp. margarine, then wrap in banana leaf. Bake at 375° F. for 30 minutes. Remove wrappings, brush with 1 tbsp. margarine, bake 20 minutes more. Put in a platter, garnish with tomato slices and spring onion. Serve with the sauce. Makes 6 servings.

Sauce

1 c. Carnation Evaporated Milk strained*   ½ tsp. Aji-no-moto
2 tbsps. margarine

Combine above ingredients in a saucepan. Cook over low flame until thick. Serve with the fish.

* *Carnation Evaporated Milk strained from tomatoes, onions and calamansi.*

GAMBAS

½ k. med. sized live shrimps
5 cloves garlic, chopped fine
¼ c. olive oil or cooking oil
Dash of hot chili sauce

1 tbsp. lemon juice or
   calamansi juice
½ c. white wine
1-2 tbsp. bread crumbs
Green olive for garnishing

Prepare Spanish Tomato Sauce. Set aside. Shell and devein shrimps. Set aside. Brown garlic in olive oil. Drop shrimps, toss until pink. Add lemon juice, wine, and hot chili sauce. Spoon 2 tbsps. Spanish Sauce. Cook 1 minute more. Thicken with 1 to 2 tbsps. bread crumbs if necessary. Serve hot on a mound of rice. Garnish with olives.

Spanish Tomato Sauce

¼ c. olive oil
1 clove garlic, crushed

½ c. onion, chopped fine
1 c. tomato sauce

Saute garlic and onion in olive oil. Add tomato sauce. Simmer gently for ½ to 1 hour.

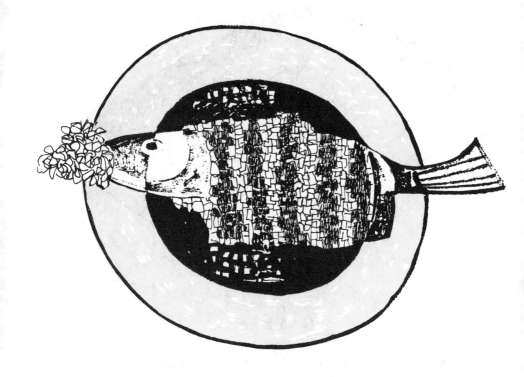

LAPU-LAPU RELLENO

1 k. lapu-lapu or any white
    meat fish
2 hard cooked eggs, sliced
4 slices cooked ham
¼ c. flour
½ c. olive oil

1 clove garlic
1 tbsp. calamansi or lemon
    juice
Sprig of parsley for
    garnishing
Stuffed green olives

Prepare Spanish Tomato Sauce.*   Set aside.   Clean fish.   Slit at the
back to open and debone.   Stuff with alternate layer of egg and ham.
Tie with string.   Dredge in flour and put in a baking pan.   Set aside.
Heat olive oil and fry the garlic.   Pour over fish.   Bake at 350°F. until
half done.   Baste occasionally with pan oil.   Remove pan from oven.
Pour Spanish Tomato Sauce, calamansi or lemon juice.   Return to
oven, bake 15 minutes longer.   Arrange on a platter, garnish with parsley and chopped olives.   Serve hot.

Recipe of Spanish Tomato Sauce, on page 56.

40

ALMEJAS CON SALZA VERDE

2 cloves garlic, crushed
1 onion, chopped
2 tbsps. olive oil
¼ c. parsley, chopped
1½ c. clam broth
2 hard cooked eggs, chopped

½ c. green peas
50 pcs. halaan or clams, boiled briefly
1 tsp. salt
1 tsp. Aji-no-moto
⅛ tsp. pepper
2 tsps. cornstarch dispersed in
water

Saute garlic and onions in olive oil.   Add parsley and broth.   Blend in chopped eggs and peas.   Cook 1 minute.   Add halaan.   Season with salt, Aji-no-moto and pepper.   Thicken with cornstarch.   Serve hot.

PESCADO AL HORNO

⅓ c. calamansi or lemon juice
1 tsp. salt
1 tsp. pepper
⅛ tsp. paprika
1 c. olive oil
1 c. tomato sauce

1 Lapu-lapu or Bacoco
¼ k. medium-sized shrimps
¼ c. bread crumbs
½ c. grated cheese

Prepare marinade by combining calamansi juice, salt, pepper and paprika. Set aside. Clean fish. Set aside. Shell shrimps leaving tail. Let fish and shrimps stand in the marinade for 15 minutes. Prepare stuffing.

Stuffing

1 red pepper, diced
1 onion, sliced

1-2 tsps. sugar
1 tsp. salt
⅛ tsp. paprika

Combine ingredients together. Stuff stomach of fish. Dredge fish and shrimps in bread crumbs. Arrange on a baking sheet, pour olive oil and tomato sauce. Garnish with onion rings and pepper strips. Sprinkle generously with bread crumbs and cheese. Bake at 350°F. 45 minutes or until done. Baste occasionally. Serve right on the baking sheet. Garnish with sprigs of parsley.

PRAWNS IN TOMATO SAUCE

½ k. prawns

¼ c. cornstarch

¼ c. cooking oil

4 stalks leeks, cut in 1" piece

1 c. tomato sauce

½ c. water

1½ tbsps. sugar

1 tsp. salt

With a kitchen scissor, snip the legs and tails of the prawns. Cut in 1" diagonal pieces. Dredge in cornstarch and fry until crisp. Set aside. Saute the leeks and the rest of the ingredients. Simmer until thick, then add fried prawns. Simmer until sauce is almost dry.

GAMBAS A LA PLANCHA

500 gms. fresh medium-sized
   shrimps, in shell
2 tbsps. coarse salt
¼ c. olive oil

2 tbsps. chopped parsley
1 clove garlic, minced
5 tbsps. olive oil or cooking
   oil

Toss shrimps and coarse salt together. Heat a heavy skillet until very hot. Drop shrimps and stir to keep from sticking. Cook 1 minute, then add 4 tbsps. olive oil. Cook 3 minutes more. Transfer to a platter. Mix parsley, garlic and 1 tbsp. olive oil. Serve with shrimps.

SHRIMPS IN WINE SAUCE

½ k. fresh shrimps, shelled and
   deveined
¼ c. flour
¼ c. olive oil
¼ c. dry white wine
1 tsp. tomato paste

2 tbsps. warm water
½ tsp. salt
¼ pepper
Dash of cayenne pepper
1 tbsp. chopped parsley
1 tbsp. spring onion, chopped

1 tsp. lemon or calamansi juice

Dredge shrimps in flour. Heat olive oil in a skillet. Put in shrimps, toss until pink. Drain. Combine drained olive oil, white wine, tomato paste, water, salt, pepper and cayenne pepper in a saucepan. Cook mixture over low heat for 1 minute. Add sauteed shrimps, parsley and spring onions. Cook 5 minutes more. Add lemon juice. Serve hot.

ROYAL APAHAP

1 apahap, lapu-lapu or red
   snapper (about 1 kilo)
1 tsp. salt
1 c. mayonnaise*

¼ tsp. pepper
4 onions, cut in rings
2 tbsps. olive oil
¼ c. water

Season fish with salt and pepper. On a baking dish, arrange a bed of onion rings, lay fish, garnish with more onions. Dribble with olive oil and water. Bake at 350°F. for 20 minutes. Prepare sauce.

Sauce

2 cloves garlic, crushed
1 onion, minced

1 c. tomato sauce
2 tbsp. olive oil

Saute garlic, onion and tomato sauce in olive oil. Simmer over low fire about 15 minutes. Remove fish from oven, add sauce. Bake for 20 minutes. Remove again from oven, cover top with Mayonnaise and bake 5-10 minutes more. Serve hot.

* *Recipe of Mayonnaise, on page 141.*

BAKED FISH

1 pc. lapu-lapu
(about 1 to 1½ k.)
1 tsp. salt
¼ tsp. freshly ground black
pepper

⅓ c. butter or margarine
1 pc. onion, chopped
2 c. bread crumbs
2 tsp. chopped sour pickles
¾ tsp. sage

¼ c. dry white wine

Preheat oven to 400°F. Clean, wash and dry fish. Cut diagonal slashes on sides of fish. Rub salt and pepper inside and outside of fish. In a skillet heat ⅓ c. butter or margarine, add the onions and brown lightly. Add the crumbs, chopped pickles, sage and half of the wine. Stuff the fish with the mixture. Sew or skewer fish. Place fish in a well-greased shallow pan lined with foil. Brush the remaining butter on the fish and pour the rest of the wine. Bake uncovered until the fish flakes easily when tested with a fork (about 40 minutes). Baste frequently with drippings or additional butter and wine. Serve with mayonaise or other desired sauce.

POACHED FISH

1 pc. lapulapu (about 1½ k.)
8-10 c. water
¾ to 1 c. vinegar
1 tsp. salt
2 pcs. carrots, minced

3 onions, minced
1 bay leaf
Pinch of thyme
4 stalks of parsley
6 pcs. pepper corn

Place all ingredients, except peppercorn and lapu-lapu into a saucepan. Bring to a boil and allow to simmer for one hour. Add peppercorns and allow to simmer for 10 minutes more. Pass through a food mill or a fine strainer. Place clean and dry lapu-lapu or other white meat fish in tepid courtbouillon and bring to a boil. Lower flame and allow to simmer until fish is cooked. May be served with hollandaise sauce or mock hollandaise sauce.

MOCK HOLLANDAISE SAUCE

3 tbsps. flour
½ tsp. salt
¼ tsp. pepper
½ c. Carnation Evaporated Milk
½ c. water or fish stock

4 tbsps. butter, beaten
4 egg yolks, beaten
¼ c. butter melted
3 tbsps. lemon juice or dayap juice

Over a low flame, blend butter and flour into a smooth paste. Add salt and pepper and stir until the mixture is smooth and bubbly. Remove from the fire and add Carnation Evaporated Milk and water or fish stock gradually. Bring to a boil for one minute while stirring constantly. After removing from the fire add eggyolks, melted butter and lemon or dayap juice. Serve warm.

Hollandaise Sauce:

3 egg yolks
1 tbsp. cold water
½ c. soft butter

¼ tsp. salt (less if butter is salty
½ to 1 tsp. lemon juice

Combine egg yolks and water in the top of a double boiler and beat with a wire whisk over hot (not boiling) water until yolks are fluffy. Add a few spoonfuls of butter to the mixture and beat continually until the butter has melted and the sauce starts to thicken. Care should be taken that the water in the bottom of the double boiler never boils. Continue to add the butter bit by bit, stirring continously. Lastly, add the salt and lemon juice. If a lighter sauce is preferred a tbsp. of hot water may be added. Sauce is served tepid, not hot. Pour over poached fish and garnish with boiled potatoes and parsley leaves.

SHRIMP CROQUETTES

300 gms. fresh shrimps*
6 tbsps. butter or margarine
6 tbsps. flour
½ tsp. salt
⅛ tsp. pepper

1 c. Carnation Evaporated Milk
1 c. water
2 eggs, slightly beaten with
   ¼ c. water
1½ c. bread crumbs

Cook shrimps, chop finely and set aside. Make Bechamel Sauce as follows: Melt butter or margarine in a skillet. When melted, blend in flour and stir well. Add salt and pepper. Pour in Carnation Evaporated Milk and water gradually into the butter-flour mixture until all the liquid is absorbed. When sauce is smooth and thick, add the chopped shrimps. Pour into an ungreased pan and let cool in refrigerator. When cold enough to be handled, divide into small portions. Shape each portion into smooth oblongs, roll in flour, eggs bread crumbs, eggs and bread crumbs again. Place in strainer and lower into hot fat. Deep fat fry. Serve hot. Makes 6 servings.

*VARIATIONS: Substitute 1 cup cooked, chopped chicken or 1 cup chopped ham or 1 cup grated cheese, for shrimps.

Meats
· Beef
· Chicken
· Pork

BEEF TERIYAKI

½ k. beef tenderloin or lean pork, sliced thin as for tapa

Sauce

¼ c. soy sauce
⅓ c. honey
1 tsp. Aji-no-moto

2 tbsps. sugar
1 clove garlic, minced
½ tsp. ginger, cut finely

Marinate beef or pork in sauce overnight in refrigerator. Turn occasionally. Bake at 350°F. for 20 minutes or until meat is done. Baste with sauce occasionally. May also be broiled over charcoal.

PEARL BALLS

½ k. ground beef
2 pcs. boiled potato, mashed
2 eggs
½ onion, chopped
1 tsp. sugar
2 tsps. soy sauce

2 tsps. ginger juice
2 tsps. salt
½ tsp. Aji-no-moto
2 c. glutinous rice, soaked
　overnight

Mix ground beef, mashed potato, eggs and onion thoroughly. Add all other ingredients except rice and mix thoroughly. Using a tablespoon, shape mixture into small balls. Drain soaked rice thoroughly and roll meat balls in it until they are well-covered. Place meat balls in steamer over wet cloth and steam for 30 minutes. Serve hot.

BEEF WITH KUTSAY

½ k. beef tenderloin
1 egg white
1 tbsp. cornstarch
1 c. cooking oil
3 tbsps. soy sauce

½ tsp. Aji-no-moto
3 tbsps. water
1 red pepper, cut in strips
¼ c. kutsay (Chinese leeks)
　cut into strips
Sesame oil

Coat tenderloin with egg white, then with cornstarch. Let stand for 15 minutes. Deep fat fry. Drain out fat. Leave 3 tbsps. fat in pan. Add the soy sauce, water and Aji-no-moto. Drop the red pepper and kutsay. Cook for 2 minutes. Before serving sprinkle sesame oil.

PUCHERO WITH EGGPLANT SAUCE

½ kilo pork liempo, cut into serving pieces
½ chicken, cut into serving pieces
½ k. beef, cut into serving pieces
2 pcs. chorizo de bilbao
6 c. water
1 tsp. salt
1 bunch green onions
1 small cabbage

⅛ k. abitsuelas (green beans)
4 pcs. potatoes
4 pcs. saba bananas
1 c. garbansos or chick peas, boiled until tender
2 tbsps. cooking oil
2 cloves garlic, crushed
1 onion, sliced
4 c. broth (from above meats)
2 tsps. Aji-no-moto
Salt to taste

Boil pork, chicken, beef, chorizo de bilbao, in water, salt, and green onions. When tender, remove and cook cabbage and green beans separately in the broth. Remove and set aside. Boil potatoes and bananas in water until tender. Remove. Cut bananas crosswise diagonally, quarter potatoes. Skin chick peas. Set aside. Saute garlic and onion in hot oil. Add broth. Bring to a boil then put in meats, bananas, potatoes, chick peas and vegetables. Season with salt and Aji-no-moto. Serve with Eggplant Sauce.

Eggplant Sauce

6 eggplants
3 cloves garlic

Salt and pepper to taste
½ c. vinegar

Broil eggplants until tender. Peel and mash. Set aside. Chop garlic finely and add to mashed eggplant. Add vinegar, salt and pepper to taste. Serve with Puchero.

SUKI-YAKI

¼ k. beef round, sliced paper
   thin then cut into 2″ squares
1 tbsp. soy sauce
1 tbsp. sugar
3 pcs. dried mushrooms,
   soaked in water, cut in half
2 cakes tokua or bean curd,
   cut 2″ squares
2 large onions, quartered
1 pc. carrot, in thin rounds
2 stalks leeks, cut 1 inch long
5-6 leaves of Baguio pechay,

cut into serving pcs.
50 gms. sotanghon or rice
   noodles (angel's hair)
   soaked then cut as
   desired
1½ tbsps. sugar
3-4 tbsps. soy sauce
½ c. beef stock or ½ c. hot
   water with 1 bouillon cube
   dissolved
1 tsp. Aji-no-moto
¼ c. butter or margarine

Marinate beef in 1 tbsp. soy sauce and 1 tbsp. sugar. Set aside. Prepare mushrooms, tokwa, vegetables and sotanghon. Combine sugar, soy sauce, stock and Aji-no-moto. Set aside. Melt butter in a heavy skillet or suki-yaki pan. Fry mushroom. Put to one side of pan. Fry beef quickly on both sides. Set aside. Add onions and tokwa.

NOTE: The different ingredients are all simmered in one pan but they should not be mixed together. Thus, the vegetables and meat are on separate mounds.

Drop in carrot rounds, cover, let simmer 1 minute. Put in pechay and leek stalks. Cook 1 minute. Add the pechay leaves, sotanghon and stock. Simmer 2 minutes more. Serve immediately on suki-yaki pan or pour in a platter. Serve hot.

BEEF WITH OYSTER SAUCE

½ k. beef tenderloin, in strips
2 tbsps. white wine
2 tbsps. cornstarch
1 tbsp. sugar
½ tsp. Aji-no-moto
¼ c. soy sauce

¼ c. cooking oil
1 onion, sliced in rings
2 tsps. oyster sauce
Frozen green peas, thawed
then boiled

Marinate beef in wine and cornstarch. Set aside. Combine sugar, Aji-no-moto and soy sauce. Set aside. Bring cooking oil to a full boil. Drop beef all at once. Cook for 5 minutes. Stir constantly. When done, drain out excess fat. Put back beef in pan, add sliced onions, soy sauce and sugar mixture. Stir 2 minutes. Remove from the fire. Flavor with oyster sauce Garnish with green peas. Serve immediately.

BEEF CORDON BLEU

½ k. beef tenderloin
Salt and pepper to taste
4 slices swiss or cheddar
cheese

4 slices cooked ham
¼ c. all-purpose flour
2 eggs, beaten
½ c. bread crumbs

¼ c. butter

Slice beef into 4 equal sizes, make a pocket in steak for filling. Season beef lightly. Lay a slice of cheese and ham inside the steak. Seal edges. Dredge in flour, dip in egg, roll in bread crumbs. Fry in butter about 4-5 minutes on each side. Garnish and serve.

CHATEAUBRIAND

1 k. beef tenderloin, trimmed
Salt
Maggi sauce
Pepper
½ lb. butter, in chunks

1 can sugar peas
½ can mushrooms, sauteed in butter
½ k. sliced potatoes, fried in butter

Season beef with salt, maggi sauce and pepper. Grill both sides until medium done. Slice, transfer to a platter. Dot with chunks of butter over hot meat. Serve with buttered green beans, carrots and potatoes. Serves 6.

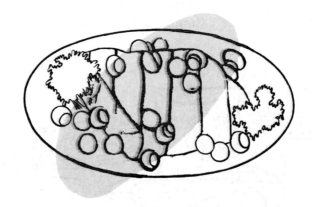

CALDERETTA

½ k. pierna corta, (beef round) cut in serving pieces
¼ c. vinegar
10 pcs. peppercorn, crushed
1 tsp. salt
2 cloves garlic, crushed
¼ c. cooking oil

1 c. onion, sliced
½ c. tomato sauce
1½-2 c. boiling water
1 c. red or green pepper, cut in strips
1 pc. laurel or bay leaf
Dash of hot sauce

⅓ c. liver spread

Marinate beef in mixture of vinegar, peppercorn, salt and crushed garlic for 1½-2 hours. Fry pieces of beef in cooking oil. Add onions and saute until tender. Pour in tomato sauce and boiling water. Add the green pepper, bay leaf and hot sauce as desired. Cover and simmer until meat is tender. Blend in liver spread. Cook 5 minutes more. Serves 5.

ITALIAN SPAGHETTI

Tomato Meat Sauce:

2 tbsps. cooking oil
2 tbsps. butter
2 onions, chopped
1 stalk celery, chopped
100 gms. ground pork
½ k. ground beef (round)
2 tbsps. vino blanco
3 large clove garlic, finely chopped

1 bay leaf
Dash of pepper
1½ c. tomato sauce
½ tsp. salt
½ tsp. Aji-no-moto
⅛ c. grated cheese
1½ c. beef stock

Heat cooking oil, add butter. Cook chopped onions slowly until tender. Add celery. Add ground pork and cook 10 minutes. Then add beef, wine, garlic and spices. Allow to cook for 5 minutes and add the tomato sauce.. Correct seasoning. Allow to simmer gently for an hour or until thick. A little flour maybe added if the sauce is too thin.

For Spaghetti:

1 box spaghetti — 8 oz.

Measure 8 c. water in a pan. Add 1 tbsp. cooking oil and 1 tsp. salt. Let boil and add spaghetti. Bring back to boil. Spaghetti may be done in 8-10 minutes. It is best not to overcook. When done, drain on a colander and add butter to prevent lumping.

BEEF WITH FRIED NOODLES

½ k. beef tenderloin, in strips
2 tbsps. white wine
2 tbsps. cornstarch
1 tsp. sugar
½ tsp. Aji-no-moto
¼ c. soy sauce
2 c. cooking oil for deep fat frying

¼ c. stock
4 pcs. dried mushrooms
2 tsps. oysters sauce
1 c. togue, long, both ends trimmed off
½ k. noodles, (not dry)
Frozen green peas, cooked
Sesame oil

Measure 8 c. water in a pan. Add 1 tbsp. cooking oil and 1 tsp. salt a full boil. Drop beef all at once. Cook for 5 minutes. Stir constantly. When done, drain out excess fat. Put back beef in pan, add sliced onions, soy sauce, sugar and Aji-no-moto. Stir 2 minutes. Remove from the fire. Flavor with oyster sauce. Add long togue. Cook one minute. Fry noodles in portions, browning bottom and top (like pancakes). Arrange on platter. Pour beef mixtures on top. Garnish with green peas. Sprinkle with a few drops of sesame oil and serve.

COCIDO
(Spanish Boiled Dinner)

½ k. beef shank (bias)
1 k. soup bones
1 chicken (about 1 k.)
½ k. lean pork (pigue)
1 tsps. peppercorn
3 pcs. tomatoes, quartered
3 stalks leeks (about 200 gms.
3 onions, quartered
1 head garlic, crushed
3 tbsps. olive oil
¼ k. string beans

200 gms. slab bacon, cut in chunks
3 pc. chorizo de bilbao
1 morcilla or Spanish blood sausage
¼ k. potatoes
¼ k. cabbage
¼ k. Baguio pechay or Chinese cabbage
2 pcs. carrots

Boil beef and soup bones with, 1 stalk leek, 1 tsp. peppercorn, tomato and onion. When beef is tender, remove and cut into serving pieces. Set broth aside. Boil chicken and pork separately with the same ingredients. When tender, remove and set broth aside. Prepare Spanish Tomato Sauce. Heat olive oil. Brown bacon slightly. Pour Spanish Tomato Sauce, combined beef, chicken and pork broth. Let boil. Add softened meats, chorizo de bilbao and morcillas. Simmer. In another pan, cook vegetables until half done in beef and chicken broth. Add to meats, cook until done. Arrange on a platter. Serve with broth and Spanish Tomato Sauce.

Spanish Tomato Sauce

¼ c. olive oil
3 cloves garlic, crushed
4 large onions, chopped
1 c. tomatoes, chopped

1 c. tomato sauce
1 c. broth
Salt and pepper
Aji-no-moto

Saute garlics, onions and tomatoes in olive oil. Cook till tender. Add tomato sauce and simmer for 10 minutes. Add broth and seasonings. Cook slowly for 1 hour in a covered container.

DELICIOUS HAMBURGER

½ k. beef, ground round
1 egg, raw
½ tsp. mustard
1-2 tbsps. Worcestershire Sauce

¼ tsp. salt
⅛ tsp. pepper
1 slice loaf bread
¼ c. Carnation Evaporated Milk

½ tsp. Aji-no-moto

Tear break into pieces and soak in ¼ c. Carnation Evaporated Milk. Add pepper, salt, Aji-no-moto, Worcestershire sauce, egg and mustard. Add mixture to ground beef and knead. Mix well. Pat according to desired shape. Pan fry in a mixture of hot oil and butter. Serve hot.

BATANGAS ADOBO

½ k. beef
200 gms. beef heart
100 gms. beef liver
½ k. pork

½ to 1 c. vinegar, depending on
    acidity
1 small head garlic
½ tsp. black pepper
1 tsp. salt

3 tbsps. atsuete soaked in 1 c. warm water*

Cut all meats into serving pieces. In a saucepan, combine vinegar, garlic, pepper, salt. Put in beef and beef heart. Let cook for 20 minutes. Add pork, beef liver and atsuete water and simmer until tender. Strain sauce. Brown the garlic and then the meats in hot oil. Return to saucepan. Cover and simmer until sauce thickens.

See glossary page 211.

PEPPER STEAK A LA CREME

1 pc. tenderloin (about 1 kilo)
¼ c. butter
¼ c. rich beef stock

½ to 1 tsp. salt
2 tbsps. whole black pepper,
    freshly pounded
½ c. sour cream

Trim tenderloin and coat with salt and pepper. Heat butter in heavy frying pan and brown tenderloin. Transfer to baking dish and roast in 320° oven for 20 minutes or until done to desired stage. Remove meat from pan and set in warm place. Dissolve all drippings in pan with beef stock. Add to heavy frying pan where tenderloin was browned Heat thoroughly and add sour cream. Slice tenderloin and pour sour cream sauce on top. Serve hot.

CONTINENTAL BEEF ROLL

1 k. beef kalitiran, (whole,
sliced ½ inch thick)

Filling

¼ k. lean pork, ground
½ c. cooked ham, chopped
2 hard cooked eggs, chopped
¼ c. mushroom, chopped
   (save liquid)
¼ c. onion, chopped
2 tbsps. quaker oats or bread
   crumbs

1 tbsp. parsley, chopped
1 tsp. Aji-no-moto
1 tbsp. worcestershire sauce
1 tsp. maggi sauce
¼ c. grated cheese
1 tsp. salt
¼ tsp. pepper

Sauce

1 c. water &
   mushroom juice
1 onion, sliced
1 tbsp. maggi sauce
1 tbsp. worcestershire sauce

½ tsp. salt
⅛ tsp. pepper
2 tbsps. margarine
2 tbsps. flour
¼ c. sliced mushrooms

¼ c. cooked ham, diced finely

Flatten meat with a mallet. Set aside. Mix ingredients for filling and spread on meat. Roll. Tie with string to secure. Brown in hot cooking oil. Transfer to a baking pan. Add water, mushroom juice, onion, maggi, worcestershire sauce, salt and pepper. Brush top with margarine. Cover with foil and bake at 350°F. for 2 hours or until tender. Meanwhile, prepare garnishing.

Garnishing

2 tbsps. butter
1 large potato, boiled then
   sliced or 10 tiny potatoes
   boiled

1 carrot, boiled then cut in
   rounds
1 tbsp. parsley, chopped

Melt butter in a pan. Saute potatoes and carrots. Sprinkle with chopped parsley. Set aside. When meat is ready, slice, then arrange on a platter. Pour sauce into a saucepan. Reduce. Thicken with flour. Add ham and mushroom. Spoon sauce over sliced meat and garnish with carrots and potatoes.

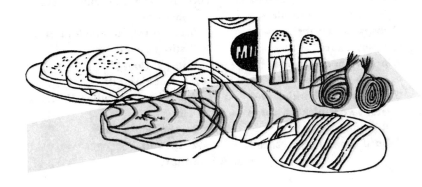

MEAT LOAF DE LUXE

1 egg, beaten	1 c. soft bread, about 4 slices
¾ c. Carnation Evaporated Milk	cut in pcs.
1 tsp. AJI-NO-MOTO	½ c. onion, minced
1½ tsps. salt	½ k. pork ground
Dash pepper	½ k. beef, ground
4-6 strips bacon	

Combine egg, Carnation Evaporated Milk, Aji-no-moto, salt, pepper and bread. Add onions, ground pork and ground beef. Mix well. Line a loaf pan (8" x 5" x 3") with bacon across width of the pan. Pack meat mixture into the pan. Bake in moderate oven, 350°F., 1½ hours. Remove from oven. Invert meat loaf in a baking sheet, raise oven temperature to 450°F. or broil. Return meat loaf to broiler for about 10 minutes, to brown bacon. Makes 8 servings. Serve with catsup or gravy.

Gravy

Drippings (about ⅓ c.)	1 bouillon cube
2 tbsps. flour	Salt
1 c. hot water	

Put drippings in a saucepan. Add flour. Cook until flour is well blended in the drippings. Add water wherein the bouillon cube was dissolved. Cook until done. Taste and correct seasoning.

MORCON

1 k. beef, sliced as for morcon, ¾" thick, in one piece
2 tbsps. calamansi juice
¼ c. soy sauce
4 pcs. vienna sausage, cut into 4 diagonally
2 pcs. sweet gherkins or 4 pcs. sweet pickles, cut in thin long strips
2 hard cooked eggs, sliced

100 gms. cheddar cheese, cut in strips
½ pc. carrot, cut into long strips
3 slices bacon
2 tbsps. flour
¼ c. cooking oil
3 pcs. bouillon cubes dissolved in
3 c. boiling water
¼ tsp. salt
½ tsp. Aji-no-moto

Marinate beef in calamansi juice and soy sauce. Arrange strips of vienna sausage, sweet gherkins, hard cooked eggs, cheese, carrots and bacon on marinated beef. Roll neatly and tie with a string. Dredge in flour then brown in hot cooking oil. Transfer to a big saucepan. Add bouillon water. Season with salt and Aji-no-moto. Cover and simmer until beef is tender. Slice, arrange in a platter. Pour sauce on top. Garnish with sprigs of parsley. Serves 10.

BEEF WITH MUSTASA LEAVES
(5 servings)

½ c. cooking oil
½ k. beef sirloin, cut in strips
⅓ c. toyo

⅓ c. water
3 c. mustasa leaves (buro) salted
3 drops sesame oil

Saute the beef in oil. Cover for 3 minutes. Add the toyo and the mustasa leaves. Stir and cook for 8 to 10 minutes. Correct seasoning. Serve hot.

MECHADO A LA ANGELES

1 k. beef
  (kabilugan) larded with 4-6
  strips of pork fat
4 big onions, quartered
¾ c. tomato sauce
½ c. soy sauce

2 c. beef stock or 2 cubes beef
  bouillon and 2 c. water
1 pc. bay leaf
4 potatoes, quartered and fried
¼ c. oil

In a deep heavy saucepan, heat oil. Place meat and brown on all sides. Add rest of the ingredients. Add fried potato quarters and continue cooking till done. Slice and serve hot with the sauce.

STUFFED SWEET GREEN PEPPERS OR EGGPLANTS

4 red or green sweet pepper
  (siling Baguio)
3 cloves garlic, macerated
5 tbsps. oil
1 large onion, chopped
2 tomatoes, chopped

¼ c. — ½ c. pork stock
½ k. ground pork
  Salt and pepper
2 eggs beaten, seasoned with
  salt and pepper

Boil sweet pepper; set aside. Saute garlic, onion, tomatoes and ground pork in hot fat. Add stock. Season with salt and pepper. When done, remove from fire and cool. Mix part of beaten egg with meat mixture. Sweet pepper: Remove top portion and fill with meat mixture. Boil or broil eggplant. Peel. Split and spread fan like. Top with cooked ground pork and spread over surface. Cover with beaten eggs. Lay stuffed eggplant till top is golden brown. Dip in well beaten eggs. Fry; drain and serve hot. Serves 4.

MECHADO

1 k. beef kabilugan, whole
¼ c. cooking oil
4 cloves garlic
1 onion, sliced
2 pcs. potatoes quartered, fried
1 carrot, cut in ½" round
1 slice dayap or lemon with

rind
2 tbsps. soy sauce
½ tsp. peppercorn
1 c. tomato sauce
1 pc. laurel leaf
1 tsp. salt
1½ c. hot water

Brown meat in cooking oil. Set aside. In the same oil, saute garlic and onion. Cook 5 minutes. Put in dayap, soy sauce, peppercorn, tomato sauce, laurel leaf and salt. Simmer a few minutes more. Add water, cover and simmer. Add potatoes and carrot, when meat is tender. Slice meat. Arrange on a platter with the vegetables. Strain sauce, pour over meat.

NOTE: Use cooked green beans, fried potatoes and cubed boiled carrots for garnishing.

BEEF STROGANOFF

½ k. round steak, cut in
strips
½ c. all-purpose flour
2 tbsps. butter or margarine
½ c. chopped onion
1 clove garlic, minced
½ c. mushrooms, sliced

Mushroom juice
1 c. sour cream*
1 c. tomato sauce
½ tsp. hot sauce
½ tsp. salt
¼ tsp. black pepper
¼ c. grated gruyere cheese,
optional

Coat meat strips with flour. Brown in butter or margarine. Push to one side of pan. Saute onion, garlic and mushrooms. Stir mixture together, cover pan and simmer for 5 minutes. Combine mushroom juice, sour cream, tomato sauce and seasonings. Pour over meat. Simmer about 30 minutes or until tender. Sprinkle with grated cheese, and brown, if desired. Serves 4-6.

To 1 c. Carnation Evaporated Milk add 1 tbsp. pineapple vinegar or calamansi juice. Let stand until curdled.

MOCK CHATEAUBRIAND

1 k. beef kalitiran   ½ c. minced onion
¼ c. butter, in chunks

Lay meat on aluminum foil. Add onion and butter. Wrap. Bake at 375°F. until tender. About 1 hour. Meanwhile prepare Sauce.

Sauce

¼ c. butter or margarine   1 can mushrooms, sliced
½ c. minced onion   1 tbsp. worcestershire sauce
1 c. tomato sauce   ½ c. white wine
  Water from 1 can   1 tsp. Aji-no-moto
  mushrooms

Saute onion in butter or margarine. Add tomato sauce and simmer for 10 minutes. Pour in rest of ingredients except mushrooms. Finally add the sliced mushrooms. Simmer 5 minutes more. Slice meat, arrange in pyrex dish. Pour sauce, bake in moderate oven for 10 minutes. Serve hot.

ROAST BEEF

1 tsp. salt
½ tsp. pepper

2-3 k. rolled or standing rib
roast

Rub meat with salt and pepper.   Roast at 300°F. 25-30 minutes per ½ kilo.   Serve with gravy, mashed potatoes and sweet green peas.

Gravy

¼ c. drippings
3 tbsps. all-purpose flour
2 c. bouillon broth or beef
   stock

Salt and pepper
1 tsp. Maggi seasoning
Aji-no-moto
½ c. mushroom, sliced

Heat drippings, blend in flour. Stir in broth gradually to make medium thin sauce.   Taste and add seasoning accordingly.   Finally add sliced mushrooms.   Serve hot with roast.

BRINGE

2 tbsps. chorizo de bilbao fat
or cooking oil
2 cloves garlic, chopped
1 onion, sliced
1 chicken (about 1 k.), cut in
serving pcs.
1 pc. chorizo de bilbao, sliced
Salt to taste
1 tsp. pepper
2 tbsps. patis

3 tbsps. juice of dilaw*
(tumeric)
½ c. malagkit or glutinous rice,
washed
1¼ c. rice, washed
3½ c. coconut milk from 1
coconut, grated
1 bay leaf
Banana leaves
2 pcs. pimientos morrones, in
strips

1 hard cooked egg, in wedges

Saute garlic and onions in chorizo de bilbao fat. Drop chicken pieces and chorizo. Season. Simmer 5 minutes. Add dilaw juice and let simmer 5 minutes more. Blend in washed malagkit and rice. Pour coconut milk and cook until absorbed by rice. Stir, to prevent burning at bottom of pan. Drop bay leaf, cook 2 minutes more. At this point, transfer ½ of mixture into a skillet. Cover both pans with banana leaves and continue cooking. Allow rice to cook covered in 350°F. oven. Serve in a platter, garnished with egg wedges and pimiento strips.

PEPITORIA

Blood of one chicken or ½ c.
pork blood, strained
1 tbsp. vinegar
1 live chicken (about 1 k.)
1 head garlic, chopped

½ c. onion, chopped
1 c. tomatoes, chopped
1 c. thick coconut milk or
water (as desired)
1 tsp. salt

1 tsp. Aji-no-moto

Collect chicken blood in container with vinegar to prevent coagulation. Set aside. Dress and clean chicken. Cut into serving pieces and set aside. Heat cooking oil in pan. Saute garlic and onions. Add tomatoes. Add chicken meat, cover, and simmer until done. Uncover, pour in chicken blood mixture or pork blood stirring constantly so blood will not curdle. When blood is cooked, stir in the thick coconut milk. Boil for a few seconds. Season with salt and Aji-no-moto.

NOTE: To extract 1 cup thick coconut milk: add ½ cup warm water to one coconut, grated. Put in a cheese cloth, squeeze.

* See Glossary.

PINATISANG MANOK

1 chicken	⅓ c. patis
2 tbsps. pork lard	A handful of sili leaves
Ginger root, cut into strips, about a tsp.	

This is a recipe of Don Alfonso—he suggests that young fat, native hen be used and the best patis available.

Cut chicken into serving pieces. In a heavy saucepan (with cover), heat pork fat. Saute ginger strips and add chicken pieces. Brown chicken pieces lightly and add patis. Cover pan tightly and lower flame. Allow patis to be absorbed. Watch carefully to prevent the chicken from drying. If all patis is absorbed and chicken is still not tender, add chicken stock. There should be enough liquid. When chicken is tender, add sili leaves and continue cooking for two (2) minutes more. Serve hot.

CHICKEN AND PORK ADOBO

1 c. native vinegar
1 head garlic, crushed
½ tsp. black pepper
1 bay leaf (optional)
2 tbsps. rock salt
1-4 tbsps. soy sauce

1 chicken (about 500 gms.),
  cut up
½ k. pork, cut into 1″ x 2″ pcs.
A slice of pork liver, cut
  into 1″ x 2″ pcs. (optional)
1½-2 c. water
Cooking oil for frying

In a saucepan, combine vinegar, garlic, pepper, bay leaf, rock salt and soy sauce. Put in chicken, pork and liver. Let soak for 20-30 minutes. Add water and simmer uncovered until tender. Strain sauce. Set aside. Chop liver finely. Combine with sauce. Set aside. Brown garlic, chicken and pork in cooking oil. Return everything to saucepan, cover and simmer until sauce thickens.

CHICKEN WITH CASHEW NUTS (SIMPLE VERSION)

4 spring chicken breasts
1 egg white
1 tbsp. cornstarch
Salt

Aji-no-moto
1 tbsp. soy sauce
1 tsp. sugar
½ c. cashew nuts

Dice chicken breast. Add the egg white and cornstarch. Season with salt, Aji-no-moto, soy sauce and sugar. Blend very well. Set aside. Fry cashew nuts in cooking oil until brown and crisp. Set aside. Deep fat fry chicken breast. Drain out fat. Disperse 1 tbsp. cornstarch in ¼ cup water. Add to chicken and continue cooking. Top with crisp cashew nuts. Serve.

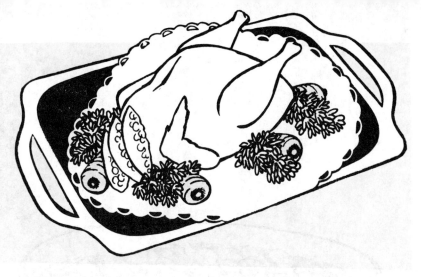

CHICKEN RELLENO (STUFFED CHICKEN)

1 large chicken, (about 1½-2
   kilos)
3 tbsps. soy sauce
2 tbsps. calamansi or lemon
   juice
½ k. ground pork
¼ k. cooked ham, chopped
   finely
4 pcs. vienna sausage,
   chopped finely

¼ c. sweet pickle relish
3 eggs
½ c. grated cheese
10 pcs. green olives, pitted
   then chopped
½ c. raisins
1-2 tbsps. tomato catsup
   Salt and pepper to taste
1 tsp. Aji-no-moto
2 hard cooked eggs, quartered

¼ c. butter

Debone chicken for stuffing. Marinate in soy sauce and calamansi juice. Set aside. Mix thoroughly next 11 ingredients. Fry about a tbsp. of the mixture. Correct seasonings. Stuff chicken, arrange quartered eggs in the center. Sew up opening and wrap in aluminum foil. Bake in moderate oven (350°F.) for 1½ hour. When almost done, unwrap and continue baking until brown. Baste with butter occasionally. Cool and slice. Arrange in a platter, serve with Gravy and Glazed Sweet Camotes.* Serves 12.

Gravy

Chicken liver, gizzard and
   heart
¾ c. pan drippings
3 tbsps. flour

2 c. broth
Salt
¼ tsp. pepper
1 tsp. Aji-no-moto

Boil chicken giblets in 2½ cups water. Reduce to 2 cups. Chop giblets, set aside. Heat pan drippings, blend in flour and brown slightly. Add chopped giblets, pour in broth stirring constantly. Cook until thick. Taste and correct seasoning. Serve with Stuffed Chicken.

* Recipe of Glazed Sweet Camote, on page 91.

DICED CHICKEN BREAST WITH CASHEW NUTS

4 pcs. chicken breast, diced	2 tbsps. rice wine
1 egg white	1 tsp. salt
1 tbsp. ang-chow (optional)	1 tsp. Aji-no-moto
½ c. bamboo shoots, diced	⅓ c. cashew nuts
1 tbsp. sugar	⅓ c. cooking oil
1 tbsp. cornstarch	4 pcs. dried mushrooms,
1 tbsp. cooking oil	soaked and then diced
1 tbsp. soy sauce	1 tbsp. soy sauce

Sesame oil

In a bowl, combine the chicken breast, egg white, ang-chow, bamboo shoots, sugar, cornstarch, cooking oil, soy sauce, rice wine, salt and Aji-no-moto. Blend thoroughly. Fry the cashew nuts in cooking oil until crisp and golden brown. Set aside. Saute mushrooms in cooking oil. Add 1 tbsp. soy sauce. Pour in the chicken mixture. Cook 5-6 minutes. Sprinkle with sesame oil. Serve hot with fried cashew nuts on top.

GINGER & ONION CHICKEN

1 chicken (about 800 gms.), cut up
1 tsp. salt
½ tsp. Aji-no-moto
¼ tsp. pepper
¼ c. all-purpose flour
½ c. cooking oil
¼ c. ginger, minced
¼ c. spring onion, minced
2 tbsps. soy sauce
2 tbsps. sugar
2 tsps. cornstarch

Combine salt, Aji-no-moto and pepper. Season chicken. Dust with flour. Heat oil. Fry four or five pieces of chicken at a time until brown. Remove chicken to a casserole. Set aside. Saute ginger and spring onion. Stir in soy sauce, sugar and 2 tsps. cornstarch dispersed in water. Bring to a boil. Pour over chicken. Add 1 c. water. Cover tightly, and simmer for 15 minutes or until chicken is done. Serve with hot rice.

PAPER-WRAPPED CHICKEN

2 tbsps. soy sauce
8 pcs. spring onion, cut finely
2-3 slices ginger, chopped finely
1 tsp. salt
2 tsps. sugar
1 tbsp. rice wine or any other cooking wine
2 spring chicken
20 pcs. (4" x 4") cellophane paper
Cooking oil

Prepare marinade by combining soy sauce, spring onion, ginger, salt, sugar and wine. Set aside. Remove bones and skin of chicken. Cut into 2" strips. Soak the sliced chicken in the marinade for 20 minutes. Then divide chicken into 20 portions. Wrap and seal each portion in a piece of cellophane paper. Heat the cooking oil and fry the packages in deep hot fat for 2 minutes. Fry in 4-5 lots if frying pan is too small to fry in one lot. Heat the oil to boiling before frying the rest. Serve hot without unwrapping the cellophane paper so that the juice and heat are sealed in.

CHICKEN CURRY

1 coconut, grated	1 chicken (about 1 k.), cut up
1½ c. warm water	1-2 tbsps. curry powder
2 tbsps. cooking oil	1 tbsp. chili powder
1 clove garlic, minced	1 tsp. salt
½ c. onions, minced	1 tsp. vetsin

¼ c. tomato sauce

Add ½ cup warm water to the grated coconut. Place in cheese cloth and squeeze to get one cup of thick coconut milk. Set aside. Repeat using 1 cup warm water. Set aside. Saute garlic and onion in cooking oil. Drop in chicken pieces, cook covered for 5 minutes. Measure curry powder, chili powder, salt and vetsin. Pour in thick coconut milk and tomato sauce. Simmer gently, stirring frequently until chicken is tender. A second cup of coconut milk may be added if needed. Dish should not be too dry. Serve with hot rice and accompaniments. Accompaniments are mango chutney, french fried onion rings, fried eggplant, chopped peanuts, crisp fried bacon chips and raisins.

MANGO CHUTNEY

1 c. vinegar	2 red peppers, julienne
4 c. brown sugar	1 head garlic, peeled
4 tsps. salt	20 pcs. native onions, peeled
4 c. green mangoes, sliced	2 hot peppers
paper thin	1 thumb-sized ginger,
2 green peppers, julienne	julienne

⅓ c. raisins

In a saucepan, combine the vinegar, sugar and salt. Boil uncovered for 5 minutes. Remove scum. Drop in sliced mangoes. Continue boiling until mangoes are transparent. Combine the rest of the ingredients except raisins. Boil until vegetables are wilted. Stir in raisins. Pack hot mixture in jars. Cover and sterilize jars for 30 minutes in pan with boiling water.

CHICKEN A LA KIEV

2 pcs. chicken breasts	Salt for seasoning chicken meat
2 pcs. drumsticks	½ c. flour
¼ lb. butter	1 c. bread crumbs
1 clove garlic, crushed	2 eggs, slightly beaten with
¼ tsp. salt	2 tbsps. water
⅛ tsp. pepper	Cooking oil for frying

Separate chicken meat from bones. Make cutlet of the breast meat and drumstick. Flatten out. Season with salt. Set aside. Combine butter, garlic, ¼ tsp. salt and pepper. In the center of cutlet, place a finger of butter mixture. Roll meat tightly. Chill thoroughly. Dredge in flour, then in slightly beaten eggs, then in bread crumbs. Repeat. Chill for at least 30 minutes. Deep-fat fry. Garnish with parsley and radish roses.

CHICKEN A LA KING

2 tbsps. butter	½ c. sliced mushrooms,
1 tbsp. flour	sauteed in butter
½ c. chicken stock	¼ c. green pepper, diced
½ c. Carnation Evaporated Milk	¼ c. pimientos, diced
½ tsp. salt	1 egg yolk, slightly beaten
1 c. boiled chicken, diced	2 tbsps. sherry

10-12 pcs. loaf bread, toasted

Melt butter in a saucepan. Stir in flour. Pour stock and scalded Carnation Evaporated Milk gradually, stirring constantly. Cook slowly until slightly thickened. Season with salt. Add the diced chicken, sliced mushrooms, green pepper and pimientos. Blend in the egg yolk and sherry. Cook until thick. Serve on toasted bread.

BREAST OF CHICKEN WITH ASPARAGUS

2 large chicken breasts or 1
chicken, boiled deboned and
cut into large squares

¼ k. cooked ham, cut into
large squares

10-12 pcs. asparagus, cut in half

Sauce

½ c. butter or margarine
1 medium onion, chopped
½ c. all-purpose flour
¾-1 c. chicken broth
Water from asparagus
2 egg yolks
1 tbsp. prepared mustard

¾ c. Carnation Evaporated Milk
2 tsps. lemon juice
Grated rind of 1 lemon
1 tsp. maggi seasoning
1 tsp. salt
1 tsp. Aji-no-moto
⅓ c. grated cheese

Saute onion in butter. Sift in the flour and blend well. Add the chicken broth stirring carefully after each addition. Add the water from the asparagus and mustard. Blend together egg yolks, Carnation Evaporated Milk, lemon juice and rind. Add to sauce. Season with maggi, salt and vetsin. Cool. In a pyrex dish, put a layer of cooked chicken, then asparagus, then the ham. Top with sauce. Repeat, ending with the sauce. Sprinkle with grated cheese. Broil until cheese is melted. Serve hot.

CHICKEN MARENGO

1 medium-sized chicken, cut
up
½ c. all-purpose flour
1½ tsp. salt
¼ tsp. pepper
¼ c. cooking oil
3 cloves garlic, chopped
¼ c. onion, chopped

½ c. tomatoes, chopped
½ c. tomato sauce
⅛ c. dry white wine or any
cooking wine
1½ c. chicken stock or water
½ c. mushroom caps
2 tbsps. cooking oil
2 tbsps. parsley, chopped

½ c. croutons

Dust chicken pieces with flour seasoned with salt and pepper. Heat cooking oil in a skillet. Fry pieces of chicken to a golden brown. Set aside. In the same skillet, saute garlic, onions and tomatoes. Pour in tomato sauce and dry white wine. Simmer 1 minute. Put back browned chicken. Add stock, cover and cook gently until chicken is tender. Meanwhile, saute mushrooms in 2 tbsps. cooking oil. Set aside. Remove chicken to a platter. Garnish with croutons and pour in sauce. Garnish with chopped parsley and sauteed mushrooms. Serve hot.

74

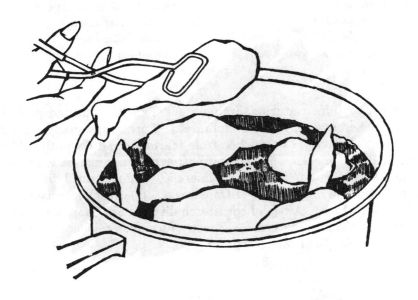

FRIED CHICKEN

1 fryer (about 1 k.), cut in serving pcs.	½ tsp. salt
	⅛ tsp. pepper
½ c. Carnation Evaporated Milk	½ tsp. Aji-no-moto
½ c. bread crumbs	1 c. cooking oil

Soak chicken in Carnation Evaporated Milk. Measure bread crumbs, salt, pepper, and Aji-no-moto in a paper or plastic bag. Put in 3-4 pieces chicken at a time and shake. Deep fat fry. Arrange on a platter, serve with buttered string beans and mashed potatoes.

POLLO A LA NARANJA

½ c. red wine
½ c. orange juice
1 tsp. paprika
1 tsp. salt
¼ tsp. pepper
1 whole chicken (about 1 k.)
½ c. olive oil

2 onions, quartered
1 bay leaf
1 sprig parsley
Peel of half an orange
1-2 c. ham bone stock
1 orange, sliced for
garnishing

¼ c. butter

In a bowl, combine red wine, orange juice, paprika, salt and pepper. Put in chicken and let stand 30 minutes. Turn occasionally. Heat olive oil and butter. Lift chicken from marinade and fry until golden brown. Place chicken, olive oil and butter mixture, marinade and remaining ingredients in a covered casserole. Simmer until chicken is tender. Arrange in a platter. Strain sauce. Pour back into casserole, simmer until thick. A tsp. of cornstarch dispersed in 1 tsp. water may be added to thicken the sauce. Spoon sauce over chicken. Garnish with orange slices and sprigs of parsley.

CHICKEN PASTEL

1 chicken (about 800 gms.),
   cut up
3 tbsps. soy sauce
   Juice of 1 lemon or dayap
5 c. cold water
1½ tsp. salt
¼ tsp. pepper
⅓ c. butter

1 pc. chorizo de bilbao, sliced
1 c. vienna sausage, sliced
1 c. broth
1 pc. carrot, cut into cubes
1 pc. potato, cut into cubes
½ c. green olives
½ c. mushrooms
2 tbsps. flour

2 hard cooked eggs, sliced

Marinate chicken in soy sauce and lemon juice. Let stand 15 minutes.
Place chicken in a saucepan, add water, salt and pepper. Simmer until
tender and almost all the water has evaporated. Set aside. Melt butter in a skillet. Brown chicken pieces. Drop in slices of chorizo de
bilbao, vienna sausage. Pour broth; cover and cook until half done.
Mix in green olives, carrots, potatoes and mushrooms. Cook everything
together. Thicken with 2 tbsps. flour if necessary. Transfer cooked
mixture to a pyrex dish, garnish with slices of hard cooked eggs. Cover
pyrex dish with pie crust.* Bake at 400°F for about 35-40 minutes or
until crust is golden brown. Serve hot.

Recipe of pastry for 1-crust pie, on page 115.

CHICKEN MEXICAN STYLE

2 chickens (about 800 gms.),
  quartered
2 tsps. salt
½ tsp. pepper
2 tbsps. maggi seasoning
½ c. flour
¼ c. olive oil
3 cloves garlic, crushed

1 c. onion, chopped
¾ c. dry red wine
¼ tsp. marjoram
2 c. water
2 pcs. chicken bouillon
¼ c. cashew nuts, fried then
  chopped
2 tbsps. sesame seeds (linga)

12 pcs. stuffed olives, sliced

Season chicken with salt, pepper and maggi seasoning. Dredge in flour. Brown in olive oil. Set aside. Saute garlic and onions in same pan. Add wine and marjoram. Simmer 15 minutes. Drop chicken, pour in water and bouillon cubes. Bring to a boil. Put in the cashew nuts, sesame seeds and stuffed olives. Simmer until done. Prepare the gravy.

Gravy

2 tbsps. butter
2 tbsps. flour

1 c. chicken broth
¼ tsp. marjoram

Melt butter. Blend in flour. Pour broth gradually, stirring constantly. Add marjoram. Combine with cooked chicken. Arrange on a platter. Garnish with fried potato balls and sprigs of parsley.

PEPITORIA II

1 large live chicken (about 1½ k.)
Combine the blood of the chicken
   with ½ c. vinegar
3 tbsps. oil
½ clove garlic, macerated

1 onion, sliced
½ c. chicken stock
1 c. coco cream (optional)
1 tsp. salt
½ tsp. pepper

Cut jugular vein of chicken and cut thru the neck of chicken. Collect blood into ½ c. vinegar. Clean and cut chicken into serving pieces. Saute the garlic, onion and chicken in the hot oil. Cover and cook for 10 minutes. Add the vinegar-blood mixture and chicken stock and cook until chicken is tender. Add coco cream and seasonings. Serve immediately for 6.

CHICKEN OR BEEF MOLE
A dish of Mexican influence

½ k. beef or chicken about 700 grms.
6 cups water
¼ rock salt
¼ tsp. pepper
1 onion cut in quarters
1 or 2 stalks celery
2-3 tbsps. cooking oil

3 cloves garlic, macerated
1 large onion, chopped
1 c. tomato sauce
2 medium size bunches pechay
   of about 100 grms.
¼ cup toasted rice, ground
¼ cup toasted peanuts, ground

Boil beef or chicken with ¼ c. rock salt, pepper, onions and celery until tender. Remove meat from broth and set broth aside. Brown garlic in hot oil and add chopped onions. Stir until onions are transparent then add tomato sauce and broth (about 4 cups). Then add the rest of the ingredients except toasted rice and peanuts. Cook the mixture and when vegetables are half cooked, add the toasted rice and peanuts. Correct seasoning. Continue cooking till meat and vegetables are done. Serve hot.

CHICKEN SAUCE SUPREME

1 fat chicken, boiled tender in
   minimum water with 1 pc.
   carrot and 2 stalks celery.
¼ c. chicken fat or butter
2-3 tbsps. flour
1 c. chicken stock, hot
¼ c. sliced canned mushrooms

2-4 tbsps. white wine
2-4 tsps. salt
   dash of white pepper
1 c. light cream
2 egg yolks
   cooked rice

Cut boiled chicken into serving pieces. Set aside. Melt fat or butter and add sliced mushrooms. Allow to cook for one minute. Then add flour and mix thoroughly. Pour hot chicken stock while stirring continuously. Allow to cook for about 2 minutes more and then add chicken, white wine and seasonings. Blend egg yolks and cream together. Remove chicken from fire and stir in yolk-cream mixture. Correct seasoning. Serve with mounds of rice.

GALLINA CON GUISANTES

1 chicken (about 1 k.)
2 c. flour
½ tsp. salt
¼ tsp. pepper
½ c. butter
¼ c. cooking oil
4 c. good chicken or beef stock
hot

2 carrots, cut in 1½ inch pcs.
3 potatoes, quartered
1 bay leaf
1 pinch oregano
1 c. green peas, canned
1 bunch leeks
1 tsp. Aji-no-moto

Mix flour salt and pepper in a paper bag. Cut chicken into serving and drop a few pieces into bag to coat each piece. Fry coated chicken in butter-oil mixture until golden brown. Add carrots and spices and leeks cut into pieces. Pour in hot chicken or beef stock. Allow chicken to cook until tender. When chicken is half done, add potatoes and green peas. The stock from the green peas may be added too. Allow chicken to cook till tender. Add ajinomoto and correct seasoning. Serve hot.

CHICKEN INDIENNE

1 chicken
1 c. flour for dredging chicken
½ tsp. salt
¼ tsp. pepper
Cooking oil
1 onion, chopped

1 tsp. sugar
1 tbsp. flour
¼ tsp. curry powder
1 c. water or chicken stock
¾ c. tomato sauce
⅓ c. Carnation Evaporated
Milk

Sift 1 c. flour with salt and pepper. Cut chicken into serving pieces. Coat chicken with salt-flour mixture by dropping chicken pieces into paper bag with salt-flour mixture. Fry chicken to golden brown. Remove chicken from pan and set aside. Saute onion in hot oil. Add sugar, flour, and curry powder. Pour in water and stir till ingredients are thoroughly blended. Add tomato sauce and chicken. Allow to simmer until tender. Correct seasoning. When almost done add 1/3 c. Carnation Evaporated Milk and serve immediately.

CREAM OF CHICKEN SOUP
Recipe on page 15

BUCO PIE
Recipe on page 190

FRIED MILK
Recipe on page 146

FISH WITH CARNATION SAUCE
Recipe on page 38

ROAST CHICKEN

1 roasting chicken (about 1½ k.), dressed	1 tbsp. calamansi or lemon juice
⅓ c. soy sauce	Butter or margarine

Marinate chicken in soy sauce and calamansi juice. Let stand 30 min. Remove chicken from marinade, stuff. Sew openings. Tuck neck by pushing in over skin. Truss wings at the side with a piece of string. Brush with margarine and wrap in aluminum foil. Bake at 325°F for 1 hour. Unwrap and continue baking until chicken is golden brown. Baste occasionally with margarine. Serve with gravy.

Bread Stuffing

⅓ c. bacon, in small pcs.	¼ c. Carnation Evaporated Milk
¼ c. chopped onions	¾ tsp. salt
2 pcs. bread, torn into pcs.	1½ tsp. Aji-no-moto
¼ tsp. pepper	

Soak break in Carnation Evaporated Milk. Set aside. Cook bacon. Set aside. In bacon fat, saute chopped onions. Add soaked bread. Put back bacon pieces. Season with salt, pepper and Aji-no-moto.

Gravy

Chicken giblet and liver	½ tbsp. flour
2 c. water or chicken stock	Drippings
2 tbsps. chicken fat	Salt and pepper to taste

Boil the chicken giblet and liver in 2 cups water until tender. Set aside 1 cup broth. Chop giblet and liver. Set aside. Heat chicken fat in a pan. Blend in flour. Pour in drippings and 1 cup stock. Add more stock if desired. Add chopped giblet and liver. Season with salt and pepper. Cook until thick.

FRIED PIGEON

⅓ c. soy sauce
1 c. water
2 tbsps. rice wine
1 tbsp. sugar
2 bay leaves

2 pigeons or squabs, dressed
1 tbsp. honey or corn syrup
Cooking oil for deep fat
   frying
¼ lemon, sliced
*Pepper-Salt

Combine first 5 ingredients together. Bring to a boil. Cook the pigeons in the above mixture for 15 minutes. Turn occasionally. Remove and cool. Rub with honey, let stand 15 minutes. Put pigeon in a strainer or frying basket. Lower basket carefully in extremely hot oil, spoon oil over. Fry 1-2 minutes. Chop pigeons to serving pieces and arrange on a platter. Garnish with lemon slices. Serve with Pepper-Salt.

*Pepper-Salt

Toss 1 tbsp. salt in a dry saucepan about 2 minutes. Add 2 tsps. black pepper. Cook until extremely hot and smoking. Serve with fried pigeon.

PATO TIM

1 duck (about 1 k.), dressed
1 tbsp. soy sauce
½ tsp. ginger, in strips
2 tbsps. rice wine
¼ c. cooking oil for frying
6 pcs. dried mushrooms,
   soaked

5 pcs. asparagus
¼ tsp. ginger, in strips
Water from 1 can of
   asparagus
2 tsps. cornstarch dispersed in
1 tbsp. water

Soak duck overnight in soy sauce, ginger and rice wine. Brown in hot cooking oil. Make a bed of mushrooms and asparagus on a platter. Sprinkle with ginger. Nestle fried duck on bed of mushrooms and asparagus and steam for 2 hours. Debone and put back on the platter. Collect drippings, add water from asparagus. Bring to a boil, thicken with cornstarch. Pour over duck. Serve hot.

CHICKEN TETRAZZINI

2 chicken (about 1 k. each),
  cut into 8 pcs.
1 can mushrooms, sliced
¼ c. butter
1 box spaghetti
3 tbsps. butter
3 tbsps. flour

2 c. chicken broth
1½-1¾ c. scalded evaporated milk
⅓ c. sherry wine
Salt and pepper to taste
½ c. grated cheese (parmesan
  or swiss)

Cover chicken with boiling water, simmer until tender. Season water. Remove chicken from the broth, shred meat finely. Set aside. Put back bones in saucepan with broth, boil until reduced to 2 cups. Saute mushrooms in butter. Set aside. Boil spaghetti in salted water "al dente." Melt butter in saucepan. Blend in flour and gradually stir in the hot strained chicken broth stirring constantly until smooth. Let boil 3-4 times. Stir in the scalded milk and wine. Divide sauce. To one part, add the shredded chicken. To another, the well-drained spaghetti and mushrooms. Season both to taste with salt and pepper. Put prepared spaghetti in a baking dish making a cavity in the center and banking it around the sides of the dish. Pour the chicken mixture in the center, sprinkle generously with cheese. Bake at 350°F. until lightly browned, about 10-12 minutes. Serve right from the baking dish.

DINUGUAN

2 tbsps. cooking oil
3 cloves garlic, minced
1 onion, minced
½ k. pork head, boiled until
soft then diced
1 pc. pork heart, boiled then
diced
100 gms. pork liver, diced

½-¾ c. native vinegar
2 c. broth
1¼ c. pork blood
1 c. beef blood
4 pcs. long green sili (hot
pepper)
1 tbsp. salt
½ tsp. Aji-no-moto

Saute garlic in cooking oil, add onion, pork head, heart and liver. Pour in vinegar and boil uncovered, without stirring until vinegar has evaporated. Add broth, cover and simmer for 15 minutes. Strain pork blood. Set aside. Cut beef blood into small pieces. Pour in pork and beef blood stirring continuously until thick. Drop sili. Simmer 5 minutes more. Season with salt and Aji-no-moto.

PORK ESTOFADO

¼ c. cooking oil
3 cloves garlic
½ k. lean pork, cut in serving
pcs.
½ c. vinegar
¼ c. soy sauce
⅓ c. sugar
½ c. water

8 peppercorns
1 carrot, cut in strips
2 pcs. saba bananas, cut
diagonally about 1" thick,
fried
2 pcs. pan de sal or french
bread, cut in squares and
fried

1 bay leaf

Brown garlic in hot oil. Drop pork pieces, fry until brown. Add vinegar, soy sauce, sugar, water, bay leaf and peppercorns. Allow to boil without stirring. Lower flame and cook until pork is almost done. Add carrots and continue cooking till pork is tender. Before serving, add fried bananas and pan de sal or French bread. Serves 5.

EMBUTIDO

½ k. lean pork, ground
½ c. vienna sausage, chopped
1½ tsps. salt
⅛ tsp. pepper
1 tsp. Aji-no-moto
2 tbsps. all-purpose flour
¼ c. sweet relish

2 eggs
¼ k. leaf lard or sinsal
1 hard cooked egg, sliced
1 pc. chorizo de bilbao, or
4 vienna sausages cut
    lengthwise into 4
¼ c. raisins

Combine first 8 ingredients. Blend thoroughly. Spread pork mixture on an 8" x 10" piece of leaf lard. Arrange slices of hard cooked eggs, chorizo de bilbao or vienna sausage and raisins on pork mixture. Roll as for jelly roll. Wrap in cheese cloth or aluminum foil. Boil in soup stock for 1 hour or if wrapped in aluminum foil, bake in a moderate oven (350°F.) for 1 hour. Chill. Before serving remove wrappings and slice. Makes 2 rolls.

HUMBA

1 k. pork pigue or pork ham,
    whole
2 cloves garlic, minced
1 c. water
2 tbsps. soy sauce
2 tbsps. brown sugar

1 tsp. salt
½ c. vinegar
1 sprig oregano
½ bay leaf (laurel)
1 heaping tbsp. tausi (salted
    black beans)

2 tbsps. fat

Mix all ingredients and cook until pork is tender. Slice pork into serving pieces. Arrange on a platter, set aside. Strain sauce and pour over pork. Serve hot.

KILAWIN

(Pickled Pork with Soybean Curd)

½ pig's head, boiled soft and
    cut into bite-size pcs.
3 pcs. tokua or soy bean
    curd, in squares and fried
1 head garlic, finely minced

1 big onion, finely sliced
½ tsp. ground black pepper or
    whole peppercorn, pounded
1 c. native vinegar
1 tbsp. soy sauce

Salt to taste

Mix above ingredients together. This may be a complimentary dish to the Pancit Luglog or served separately.

LONGANIZA

½ k. pork meat with fat,
    ground
1 tbsp. salt
½ tsp. pepper
¼ c. vinegar
½ head garlic, minced

1 tsp. paprika
⅛ tsp. saltpeter (salitre)
1 tbsp. brown sugar
1 dozen large dry pig's
    intestines (casing)

Mix first 8 ingredients thoroughly. Let stand 1-2 hours. Using funnel, fill sausage casing with pork mixture. Tie at 6" intervals and dry in the sun. Keep refrigerated. To cook: Boil sausages in enough water to cover until water has evaporated. Prick several times with a fork. Put in 2 tbsps. cooking oil. Fry until done.

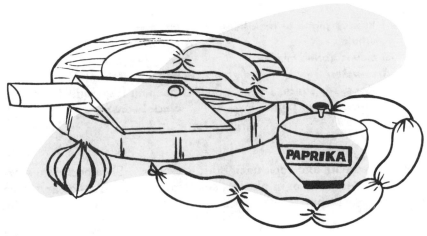

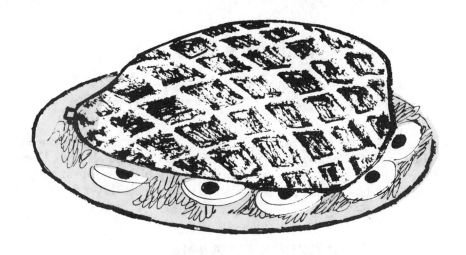

HOME-MADE HAM

1 k. pigue or pork ham, whole   3 tbsps. sugar
3 tbsps. salt   1 tsp. saltpeter (salitre)

Combine salt, sugar and saltpeter.   Spread one-half of curing mixture all over fresh pork.   Store in refrigerator in a covered container.   The next day spread the other half of the curing mixture on the meat.   Allow to stand in the refrigerator for one week.   Remove rind and tie to make a nicely shaped ham.

To Cook Ham

1 c. sugar   1 c. pineapple juice

Place ham on a rack set on a rectangular pan.   Mix sugar and pineapple juice in a bowl.   Pour this over the meat.   Bake at 325°F. to an internal temperature of 185° as tested by a meat thermometer.   Baste every 10 minutes.   This will take about 40-60 minutes.

To Stew Ham

1 c. sugar   1 c. pineapple juice

Set a rack in a skillet or on a heavy pan and place the ham.   Mix sugar and pineapple juice.   Stew over low to medium flame for 1 hour or until the center of the ham is cooked through.

NOTE: You may add ¼ tsp. cloves and ¼ tsp. pepper for an interesting flavor.   Garnish with sliced pineapples and cherries.

LECHON KAWALI

1 k. pork belly (liempo)	2 tbsps. salt
4 c. water	2 tbsps. Aji-no-moto

Boil pork belly in water with salt and Aji-no-moto until skin can be pinched easily. Remove from fire and drain. Cool and air dry. Deep fat fry in a kawali or deep saucepan until tiny blisters appear on the skin. Chop into serving pieces and serve with Lechon Liver Sauce.

LECHON LIVER SAUCE

⅛ c. liver paste	¾ tsp. black pepper
¾ c. native vinegar or other vinegar & 1/r c. water	2 tbsps. cooking oil or lard
1½ c. water	1 head garlic, minced
½ c. sugar	6 pcs. sibuyas tagalog or shallots, sliced fine
Kasubha (wild saffron fried in hot oil or 1 bay leaf optional)	⅓ c. bread crumbs
	c. water

Mix liver paste, 1-½ c. water, bread crumbs, sugar, ½ of kasubha, laurel, salt and pepper. Blend well and set aside. Saute garlic in cooking oil. Add the onions and fry until tender. Add the liver mixture. Boil without stirring. Do not cover the saucepan. Add bread crumbs dispersed in 1 c. water. Cook till it thickens. Serve, topped with the rest of the crisp brown garlic and fried kasubha.

PAKSIW NA PATA

1 large pata or pig's feet (about 1 k.)	½ c. brown sugar
½ c. vinegar	½ c. dried banana blossoms, soaked in water
½ c. water	1 laurel or bay leaf
½ head garlic, crushed	¼ c. soy sauce
4 saba bananas, fried	

Clean pata and boil in vinegar, water and garlic. Lower heat, simmer until pig's feet is tender. Add more water as needed. Put in remaining ingredients, simmer 5 minutes more. Serve hot.

ROAST PORK DINNER (LECHON)

1½ k. pork (pigue)
1 tsp. pepper
2 tbsps. garlic, crushed
1 tsp. vestin or Aji-no-moto
2 tbsps. salt

Clean the pork, combine the seasoning.   Rub the seasoning well into the pork and let stand for one hour in a cool place.   Bake in a moderate oven (350° F.) for 1½ to 2 hours or until tender.   Serve with Lechon Sauce,* Native Achara and Candied Sweet Yams.

Native Achara

1 medium-sized green papaya, grated
1 green pepper, sliced in strips
1 red pepper, sliced in strips
1 small carrot, sliced in strips
1 small cauliflower, cut into flowerettes
1 small ginger, cut in strips
1 bunch native onions, peeled
1 small ampalaya, sliced
3 tbsps. rock salt
3 c. vinegar
1½ c. sugar
2 tsps. salt

Squeeze all the vegetables (except cauliflower) in salt, let stand for one hour then press out liquid.   Blanch the cauliflower, drain and set aside. Place all the strained vegetables in a bowl or sterilized jar.   Meanwhile, combine vinegar, salt and sugar and cook over a strong flame till boiling. Remove scum, continue boiling for another 2 minutes then pour into container with vegetables.   If achara is to be stored, seal container immediately.

Candied Sweet Yams

1 k. sweet potatoes (camote)
1 c. sugar
½ c. water
1 tsp. calamansi or orange rind
3 tbsps. margarine
Juice of 1 calamansi or orange
Salt and paprika

Pare and cut potatoes lengthwise into ½" slices.   Cook covered in boiling water until nearly tender.   Drain.   Grease baking pan.   Arrange potatoes.   Set aside.   Caramelize sugar.   Add ½ cup water.   Boil. Add the margarine.   Pour over sweet potatoes.   Sprinkle with salt, paprika, calamansi juice and rind.   Bake in moderate oven for 20 minutes.   Baste several times with syrup.

* Recipe of Lechon Sauce, on page 90.

PORK AND BEEF SINIGANG

1 tbsp. lard
2 cloves garlic, crushed
1 onion
6 medium-sized tomatoes
10 pcs. camias
1 tbsp. patis
½ k. beef (sisigangin), cut in
    serving pcs.
½ k. pork sisigangin, cut in
    serving pcs.

6 pcs. native gabi
6 c. rice water
3 c. kangkong leaves and
    tender stalks (swamp
    cabbage)
5 pcs. long sili (hot pepper)
1½ tsps. salt
1 tsp. Aji-no-moto

Saute the garlic in hot lard until golden brown.   Add the onions and
cook until they become transparent.   Put in the tomatoes and camias.
When soft, crush them and add the patis.   Drop the beef and cook
covered for 5 minutes.   Add the pork, cook 5 minutes more, turning
occasionally.   Pour in rice water and cover tightly.   Let boil.   When
boiling, reduce the heat and simmer until pork and beef become tender.   Add gabi.   When tender, drop the kangkong and sili.   Season
with salt and Aji-no-moto.   Serve hot.

PORK ASADO – CHINESE STYLE

¾ c. hot stock or water
⅓ c. soy sauce
⅓ c. brown sugar
2 tbsps. white wine

1 tsp. salt
½ tsp. Aji-no-moto
2 cloves garlic, crushed
1 k. pork pigue, whole

In a 2 qt. saucepan, combine first 7 ingredients.   Put in pork.   Cover
pan, then bring to a boil.   Lower heat and simmer until meat is tender.
Slice meat.   Serve hot with the sauce.

PORK SUAM

1 k. pork	6 pcs. whole peppercorn
3 tbsps. cooking oil	6 c. rice water
3 cloves garlic, pounded	½ k. cabbage, cut into
2 pcs. onion, chopped	approximately 2" x 3" slices
1 thumb size pc. of ginger,	2 bundles misua
sliced	1 tbsp. Aji-no-moto
¼ c. patis	1 bunch green onions

Cut pork into serving pieces. Set aside. In hot oil, brown garlic and saute onions, ginger and season with patis. Add the cut pork and turn several times. Cover until it boils in its own juice. Add peppercorn and enough rice water to make pork tender. Add previously cut cabbage. When done, add misua. Before removing add the green onions. Serves 12

PORK APRITADA

1 k. pork	2 pcs. red pepper
4 pcs. potatoes, cut into	3 pcs. tomatoes
quarters	½ c. tomato sauce
1 big onion	6 tbsps. vinegar
2 tbsps. cooking oil	1½ tsp. garlic (7-10 cloves)
3 tsp. salt	⅛ c. bread crumbs

Slice pork into individual pieces. Saute in garlic, onions and tomatoes. Season with salt. Add vinegar and let boil for 5 minutes. Then add enough water or stock to make meat tender and make up for sauce. When almost done, add sliced pepper and thicken with bread crumbs. Cook for 5 minutes thereafter. Remove from fire and garnish with fried potatoes.

FRIED QUE-KIAM

½ k. lean pork, diced
4 pcs. green onion, chopped
4 pcs. dried mushrooms,
    soaked and chopped
1 tbsp. spice powder
2 tbsps. soy sauce
½ tsp. Aji-no-moto

½ tsp. salt
1 egg
1 tbsp. cornstarch cooked in
    ¼ c. water
2 sheets of "tawpe" (dried soy
    bean milk skin)
Cooking oil for deep fat frying

3 tsps. sugar

Mix the first 9 ingredients together in a bowl.   Wet edges of tawpe
with water, trim and cut in two.   Wrap the pork mixture with tawpe
and seal with cooked cornstarch.   Deep fat fry about 8-10 minutes and
cut into serving pieces.   Serve with pickled radish*

FRIED PINSEC

½ k. ground pork
¼ k. shrimps, chopped
4 stalks of spring onions,
    chopped
1 pc. bamboo shoot, chopped
4 pcs. dried mushrooms,
    soaked and chopped

1 egg
2 tbsps. cornstarch
    Salt and Aji-no-moto
2 tbsps. soy sauce
1 tsp. sesame oil
    Cooking oil for deep fat
    frying

50 pcs. wanton wrappers**

Mix first 10 ingredients together.   Wrap and fold with the wanton
wrappers.   Deep fat fry for 3 minutes.   Serve with sauce.

Sauce

3 tbsps. soy sauce
½ tsp. shredded ginger

3 tbsps. vinegar
Few drops sesame oil

Mix all together.

Recipe of Pickled Radish, on page 119.
**Recipe of Wanton Wrapper, on page 10.*

LUMPIA SHANGHAI

¼ k. lean pork, ground
¼ k. shrimps, finely chopped
⅓ c. singcamas or
   waterchestnuts, chopped
4 pcs. dried mushrooms,
   soaked then chopped
½ c. spring onion, cut very
   finely

1 tsp. salt
¼ tsp. pepper
½ tsp. Aji-no-moto
1 egg
1 tsp. soy sauce
30-35 pcs. lumpia wrapper or egg
   roll

In a bowl, combine first 5 ingredients. Season with salt, pepper and Aji-no-moto. Blend in egg and soy sauce. Beat mixture thoroughly. At one end of a lumpia wrapper, spoon about 2 tbsps. of the pork mixture and roll tightly. Brush end of wrapper with water to seal. Cut rolls into 2″ pieces. Deep fat fry. Serve hot with Sweet and Sour Sauce.

Sweet & Sour Sauce 1

¼ c. vinegar
¼ c. sugar
¼ tsp. salt
½ c. stock or water

2 tsps. cornstarch dispersed in
1 tbsp. water
1 tbsp. cooking oil
2 tbsps. tomato catsup

Combine vinegar, sugar, salt, stock and cornstarch. Set aside. Heat cooking oil. Fry tomato catsup. Add vinegar mixture and boil until thick.

STUFFED PATA

1 whole pig's leg, deboned
⅓ k. lean pork
1 tbsp. salitre or saltpeter
2 tbsps. water
1 tsp. salt
½ c. soy sauce
2 c. water

2 tbsps. sugar
2 tbsps. rice wine or white
   wine
Some spice
1 tsp. salt
2 tbsps. cornstarch, dispersed
   in ¼ c. water

Prepare pig's leg. Set aside. Cut lean pork into large pieces. Set aside. Dissolve saltpeter in water. Add salt. Combine meat from pig's feet, lean pork and saltpeter solution. Refrigerate 1-2 days. Stuff pig's leg with lean pork. Fill pata ⅔ full only or pata will break open. Sew opening. Put stuffed pata and the rest of the ingredients except cornstarch in a saucepan and simmer 1-2 hours or until tender. Cool and slice thinly. Arrange on a platter. Thicken sauce with cornstarch. Spoon over meat. Serve.

SWEET AND SOUR PORK

½ c. all-purpose flour
2 eggs, slightly beaten
½ tsp. salt
½ k. lean pork, boiled until
  tender then cut into 1" cubes
  Cooking oil for frying
½ c. broth or water

1 c. pineapple chunks
6 pcs. sweet pickles, sliced
1 green pepper, diced
1 carrot, cut in rounds
1 clove garlic, chopped fine
Sweet-Sour Sauce
1 tbsp. cornstarch dispersed in
1 tbsp. water

Make a batter with flour, eggs and salt. Dip pork cubes in batter one at a time. Fry in hot cooking oil until golden brown. Remove and drain in absorbent paper. Return pork pieces to frying pan, add pineapple chunks, sweet pickles, green pepper, carrot, garlic and ½ cup broth. Cover and cook for 10 minutes. Prepare Sweet and Sour Sauce and pour in saucepan. Let boil uncovered for 5 minutes. Thicken with cornstarch. Serve hot.

Sweet & Sour Sauce 2

½ c. sugar
½ c. water
1 tbsp. soy sauce
1 tsp. salt
¼ c. vinegar

Combine all ingredients.

ORANGE SPARE-RIBS

⅓ c. orange marmalade
2 tbsps. peach jam
⅓ c. orange juice
1 tbsp. grated orange rind
⅓ c. soy sauce

1 tsp. Aji-no-moto
½ tsp. salt
1 k. pork spare-ribs, in
  4" x ½" pcs.

Prepare marinade by combining first 7 ingredients together. Soak spare-ribs in marinade overnight. Keep refrigerated. Bake at 350°F. with half of marinade. Use other half to baste spare-ribs. When almost done, transfer to broiler, broil until quite dry. Pile on a platter, garnish with orange slices and maraschino cherries.

FRIED LUMPIA WITH SESAME SEEDS

½ k. shrimps
2 bunches spring onions
1½ c. meat asado,*
5-8 pcs. Chinese mushrooms,
  soaked in water and cut
  into pcs.
1 c. bamboo shoots
  (labong), cubed

2 egg yolks
2 tbsps. flour
1 tbsp. rice wine
  Pepper, salt
  and Aji-no-moto
10-12 big pcs. lumpia wrapper
2 egg whites
½ c. sesame seeds

Combine first 11 ingredients together. Wrap in lumpia wrapper. Grease steamer and steam for 10 minutes. Rub with egg whites and sprinkle with sesame seeds. Cool. Fry in hot fat.

POTATO PORK PIE

¼ k. ground lean pork
¼ k. ground beef
2 pcs. chorizo de bilbao,
  chopped
12 pcs. green olives (pitted and
  chopped)
½ c. raisins

¼ k. ham, chopped
3 cloves garlic, crushed
3 tbsps. cooking oil
1 onion, chopped
1 c. tomato sauce
½ c. stock
1 tsp. Aji-no-moto

Salt and pepper to taste

Saute garlic and onion in cooking oil until tender. And tomato sauce and simmer for 5 minutes. Add chorizo de bilbao, ground pork, beef. Simmer until almost done. Add the ham, green olives, raisins, salt and pepper. Simmer until done. Add stock as needed. Spoon into pyrex dish. Set aside. Prepare Mashed Potatoes.

Mashed Potatoes

2 c. boiled potatoes
¼ c. butter

1 tsp. salt
½ c. Carnation Evaporated Milk
  scalded

Mash potatoes while hot. Add butter; season with salt. Beat in hot Carnation Evaporated Milk. Spread mashed potatoes on top of cooked mixture. Garnish with tomato catsup or tomato sauce. Bake at 350° F. until brown.

* *Recipe of Pork Asado, Chinese Style, on page 92*

PORK IN CORNBREAD RING

1 loaf bread, torn to pcs.
1 c. evaporated milk
3 whole eggs
½ c. vienna sausage, chopped

2½ c. sweet corn
Pepper, salt and AJI-NO-MOTO
½ c. melted butter

Soak bread in milk until soft. Add remaining ingredients and mix thoroughly. Pour mixture on a well-greased ring mold and put on a pan with water. Bake at 350°F. till firm. Cool then unmold on a platter. Prepare pork with sauce.

Pork with Sauce

2 tbsps. onion, chopped
2 tbsps. butter
½ k. pork tenderloin, diced
1 c. sliced mushroom
1 tsp. salt

¼ tsp. pepper
½ tsp. Aji-no-moto
¼ c. flour
¼ c. butter
2 c. broth

2 egg yolks, well beaten

Cook onions in butter. Drop pork, toss 1 minute. Add mushrooms and seasonings. Cook 5 minutes more. Set aside. Prepare sauce by browning flour. Blend in butter. Gradually pour in broth stirring constantly. Cook until thick. Add eggyolks. Blend in sauteed pork. Pour in center of mold. Garnish with strips of pimientos.

PARTY PORK & BEANS

3 c. canned pork & beans
1 pig's feet or 2½ c. cooked
   pig's feet
¾ c. broth of pig's feet

1 pc. chorizo de bilbao, sliced
1 c. potatoes, cubed
2 tbsps. onions, sliced
4 pcs. bacon

Boil pig's feet until very tender. Remove bones and cut into small cubes. Fry the bacon for a while. Don't make it crisp. Set aside. In the bacon fat, saute the onions. Add the pata, chorizo de bilbao and potatoes. Pour in the broth of the pig's feet and cook 5 minutes. Add the pork and beans. Pour in a rectangular pyrex dish. Top with the slightly fried bacon and broil until mixture is bubbly.

PORK KILAWIN

1 k. pork liempo
½ c. Del Monte Vinegar
⅓ c. soy sauce
2 med. size onions, raw,
   coarsely chopped

2 c. water
½ tsp. salt

Boil pork liempo in 2 c. water and some salt. Cook until liempo is tender and skin easily peals off. While hot cut liempo into cubes. Place in a bowl and add vinegar, soy sauce and chopped raw onions. Serve immediately.

PORK SPARERIBS

1 k. pork spareribs
⅓ c. soy sauce

⅓ c. sugar (or slightly less)
1 tbsp. Aji-no-moto

Mix soy sauce, sugar and Aji-no-moto in a bowl. Marinate pork spareribs in the mixture overnight. Keep covered in the refrigerator. Remove spareribs from the marinade and bake or broil. Baste spareribs all the while with the marinade. Serve hot.

BAKED SPARERIBS IN HONEY SAUCE

1 k. spareribs, cut in serving
  pcs.
1 onion, quartered

¼ c. soy sauce
¼ tsp. pepper
½ tsp. salt

Combine ingredients together in a saucepan. Boil 2 hours or until spareribs are tender. Drain. Arrange spareribs in a baking pan, set aside. Prepare sauce.

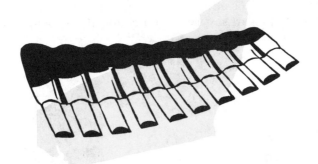

Sauce

1 tbsp. ginger juice*
½ c. honey
2 tbsps. brown sugar

1 tsp. salt
2 tbsps. soy sauce
1 onion, minced

1 tbsp. worcestershire sauce

Blend ingredients together. Pour over spareribs. Bake at 400°F. for 3 minutes. Serve with Sweet Potato-Bacon Balls.

Sweet Potato-Bacon Balls

1 k. yellow sweet potato,
  boiled and mashed
1 egg, beaten
¼ tsp. salt

¼ tsp. pepper
1 c. cooked bacon, chopped
½ c. pineapple juice
¼ c. brown sugar

Combine first 4 ingredients together. Shape into balls and roll in the chopped bacon. Arrange in a greased pan. Bake at 350°F. 15-20 minutes. Boil pineapple juice and brown sugar for 5 minutes. Use to baste sweet potato balls.

* *See glossary for ginger juice preparation.*

ALMONDIGAS WITH TOMATO SAUCE
(6 servings)

½ k. ground pork
⅓ c. flour
2 eggs beaten
Salt and pepper to taste
⅓ c. cooking oil

3 cloves garlic
1 med. onion, chopped
1 c. tomato sauce
½ c. good chicken stock

Mix the pork, flour and eggs in a bowl. Season with salt and pepper. Form into small balls. This amount will yield around 20 to 24 balls. Fry in hot oil. Set aside. In another pan saute the garlic in 1 tbsp. cooking oil. Add the onions, the tomato sauce and stock. Season with salt and pepper. Cover and cook for 10 minutes. Add the fried meat balls. Cover and cook for another 5 minutes. Serve hot.

PORK ESTOFADO II

1 k. lean pork meat, cut into
    serving pieces
¼ c. oil
½ head garlic, macerated
¾ c. vinegar
¼ to ½ brown sugar

½ c. water
1 bay leaf
1 tbsp. salt
¼ Tsp. pepper
½ tbsp. soy sauce
Banana leaf or aluminum
    foil

Fry meat in hot fat; set aside. Fry garlic to golden brown. Add meat and the rest of the ingredients. Cover saucepan with banana leaf. Seal with tight lid and simmer until meat is tender. Serve hot for 6.

PICKLED PIGS' FEET

2 Pig's feet quartered and boned
1 tbsp. soy sauce
1 tbsp. flour
1 tsp. salt
¾ brown sugar

1 cup vinegar
1 c. water
1 tbsp. rice wine
1 tbsp. Aji-no-moto

Combine all ingredients in a heavy saucepan. Cook over medium heat, simmering until tender. Remove from fire and cool. Slice before serving.

PORK APRITADA II

½ k. pork, cut into small 1½ inch cube
1 tbsp. garlic, macerated
2 tbsps. oil
½ c. onions, sliced
1 c. tomatoes, sliced fine
8 c. rice water
2 medium sized potatoes, in cubes

¼ k. ox liver sliced into 1 inch cubes
1 large sweet pepper (red or green) in strips
1 tsp. salt
¼ tsp. pepper (sliced like pork or ox liver)

Saute garlic in oil until brown. Add onions and tomatoes, cook until soft. Add pork and rice water; let simmer until tender. When tender, add sliced potatoes and cook until done. Add liver and sweet pepper, (sliced). Season and cook until liver is done, 5-8 minutes. Serve hot for 8.

THE BICOL EXPRESS

¼ c. cooking oil
1 tbsp. chopped garlic
½ c. chopped onions
¼ c. chopped or grated fresh
   ginger
2 tbsps. dilao (fresh turmeric)
1 k. pork cooked & sliced into
   ½" strips
1½ tbsp. chopped hot chili
   (siling labuyo)

1½ c. bagoong alamang
6 c. coconut cream
2-3 c. fresh hot green pepper
   (elongated variety) sliced
   diagonally ¼" strips
1½-2 c. fresh red hot peppers
   (elongated variety) sliced
   diagonally — ¼" strips
1 tsp. Aji-no-moto

Saute garlic in hot oil. Add onions and cook till translucent. Stir in fresh ginger and dilao and the sliced cooked pork. Stir continually for 5 minutes. Add bagoong alamang and chopped hot chili, (siling labuyo). Stir till the pork is completely covered by mixture. (about 15 minutes.) Pour—6 c. coconut cream and add the sliced hot green and red peppers. Continue cooking for about 20 minutes. Add the Aji-no-moto and correct seasoning. Add salt if necessary.
NOTE: Amount of chilis and hot peppers to be added according to spiciness desired.

ALMONDIGAS WITH MISUA AND EGGS
(6 servings)

50 grms. Miswa	150 grms. raw shrimps, peeled,
¼ k. grounded pork	cut diagonally
¼ c. flour	patis and pepper to taste
Salt and pepper to taste	6 c. water
1-2 tbsps. cooking oil	3 eggs, slightly beaten
	1 tsp. Aji-no-moto

Mix the pork and flour in a bowl. Season with salt and pepper and form into small balls (about 10 balls). Set aside. Saute the garlic in cooking oil until golden brown. Add the onions and the shrimps. Season with salt, patis and pepper. Add the water. When it boils add the meat balls. Don't stir. Cover and simmer for 15 minutes. Add the miswa. Add eggs into the simmering mixture and stir. More patis may be added if necessary. Cover and cook for 5 to 8 minutes more. Serve hot.

SATE BABI (INDONESIAN)

1 head garlic, crushed	½ c. brown sugar
1 tsp. black pepper (ground)	1 tbsp. rock salt
1 c. native vinegar	¼ c. soy sauce
1 k. pork, cut into 1″ cubes	

Prepare marinade by combining first 6 ingredients together. Marinate pork in mixture overnight in the refrigerator. Skewer pork pcs. in bamboo sticks. Broil over charcoal. Serve with Sate Sauce and Achara.*

Sate Sauce

½ c. soy sauce	1 hot pepper, minced
½ c. water	1 tbsp. oil
1 c. peanut butter	1 tsp. garlic
¼ c. calamansi or lemon juice	1 tbsp. chopped native
⅓ c. sugar	onions or shallots
½ tsp. macerated ginger	

Blend first 6 ingredients together. Boil until thick. Set aside. Saute garlic, native onions and ginger in hot oil. Add to thickened mixture. Add water as needed. Boil 2 minutes more. Correct seasoning.

* Recipe of Achara, on page 91

STUFFED PORK CHOPS

3 pcs. pork chops
  Juice of 3 calamansi or
    lemon juice

½ tsp. salt
¼ tsp. pepper
½ tbsp. soy sauce

½ tsp. Aji-no-moto

Stuffing

¼ c. cooked ham, chopped
2 pcs. vienna sausage,
  chopped

2 tbsps. pickle relish
¼ c. canned pineapple, cut to
  bite-size pcs.

2 tbsps. raisins

Ask butcher to cut chops into 1½″ thick pieces and make a pocket for stuffing. Prepare marinade by combining calamansi juice, salt, pepper, soy sauce and Aji-no-moto. Let pork chops stand in marinade 30 minutes. Mix ingredients for stuffing. Stuff pork chops. Wrap in aluminum foil. Bake at 350°F. for about 40 minutes or until tender. Remove from oven. Unwrap pork chops and brush with margarine. Broil about 3″ from heat till both sides are browned. Serve garnished with pineapple slices and parsley.

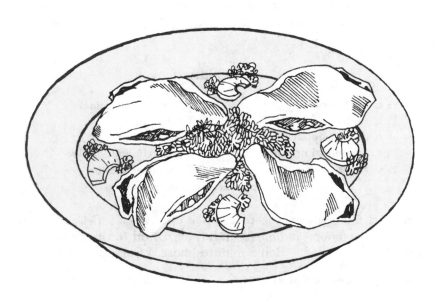

variety meats

CALLOS

1 k. goto or tripe
1 pc. "mukha ng baka" or
  cow's head
1 pc. pata de vaca (ox leg)
  Salt and vinegar
  Enough water to cover
2 stalks leeks
6-8 tomatoes
2 medium onions, quartered
4 pcs. carrots, quartered
½ c. white wine
1½ tsp. peppercorns
1½ tsp. pimenton powder
¼ c. olive oil
2 pcs. chorizo de bilbao or

Spanish sausage, sliced
200 gms. bacon, in 1" strips
1 pc. morcillas or blood
  sausage, optional
¼ c. olive oil
4 onions, sliced
2 green pepper, broiled and
  sliced
2 red pepper, broiled and
  sliced or pimientos
  morrones, sliced
¾ c. tomato sauce
  Salt to taste
  Asparagus tips and red
  pepper strips for garnishing

Clean meats with salt and vinegar. Put to a large saucepan, add enough water to cover, leeks, tomatoes, onions, carrots, white wine, peppercorns and pimenton. Cover, let boil then lower flame. Simmer until meats are tender. Heat olive oil. Drop chorizo de bilbao and bacon, fry 5 minutes. Put in morcillas, cook 2 minutes more. Set aside. Saute onions in hot olive oil. Drop in sliced peppers. Add tomato sauce and salt. Simmer 5 minutes and strain. Set aside. When meats are tender, debone and cut up into squares. Put all ingredients together in saucepan, simmer 20 minutes more. Pour into deep serving plate, garnish with asparagus tips and red pepper strips.

BACHOY

2 pcs. pork kidney (about
   300 gms.)
¼ k. pork liver
1 pc. pork heart (about 200
   gms.)
¼ k. pork lomo or tenderloin
2 segments garlic, chopped

3 tbsps. cooking oil
1 tsp. Aji-no-moto
1 tsp. patis
1 onion, chopped
1 tsp. ginger, cut finely
1½ c. water
Spring onions for garnishing
Salt to taste

Cut pork kidney, liver, heart and pork into strips. Set aside. Saute garlic in cooking oil. When golden brown add chopped onions. Cook till tender and transparent. Add pork kidney, liver, heart and lean pork. Put in ginger and continue cooking for 3 minutes. Season and cook for 10 minutes. Uncover and pour in 1 ½ cups water. Boil until meat becomes tender. Garnish with chopped green onions. Serves 6.

BINANGIS

2 tbsps. cooking oil
4 cloves garlic, minced
1 onion, chopped
½ k. pork, boiled and sliced
1 pork heart, cut into pcs.

2 pcs. pork kidney, in pcs.
¼ c. vinegar
Salt to taste
200 gms. pork liver
1 red Baguio pepper

Saute garlic, onion and pork in cooking oil. Add the heart and kidney. Season with vinegar and salt. When almost dry, add the liver, sweet pepper and cook until done.

KILAWIN NA LIBRILLO AT LABANOS

1 k. librillo or tripe
1 c. vinegar
2 c. water
1 tbsp. salt
1 head garlic, crushed

1 onion, chopped
6 pcs. tomatoes
1 c. water
4 pcs. white radish, sliced
1 tsp. Aji-no-moto

Boil tripe in vinegar, water, salt and garlic until tender. Cut to bite-size pieces. Saute onion and tomatoes. Add tripe and water. Drop radish and simmer until tender. Season with salt and pepper.

LENGUA ESTOFADA Batangas Style

1 ox tongue	1 tsp. garlic
1 onion	1 c. vinegar
5 pepper corn	¼ c. soy sauce
1 carrot	1½ c. beer
parsley	2 tbsps. worcestershire sauce
1 bay leaf	2-4 tbsps. sugar
green onion	Fried saba bananas (optional)
	Fried sweet potatoes (optional)

Clean and trim tongue and boil in 6 c. water with 1 onion quartered, 5 pepper corn, 1 carrot, sprig of parsley, 1 bay leaf and green onion, salt. Cut tongue into 1½ cubes. In a deep saucepan, add the oil and let the tongue brown. Add the garlic, vinegar, soy sauce, beer, worcestershire sauce and let tongue simmer until tender. Thicken sauce with bread crumbs and serve with fried bananas and sweet potatoes. Serve hot for 6.

LIVER IN SOY SAUCE

½ k. ox liver, sliced	6 slices bacon
½ c. soy sauce	2 large onions sliced into rings
1-2 tbsps. kalamansi juice (or lemon juice)	

Marinate liver in soy sauce and kalamansi or lemon juice. Pan fry bacon and set aside. In the bacon fat, saute onions; set aside. Cook liver in remaining hot fat (about 2-3 minutes per side). When done, add the marinade and garnish with bacon and onions rings.

DINUGUAN II
(7 servings)

½ k. pork
3 c. water with ½ tsp. salt
½ c. pig's blood
½ c. cow's blood
4 tbsps. cooking oil

1 tbsp. garlic pounded
½ c. onions sliced fine
½ c. tomatoes chopped
1 radish finely sliced
1 c. vinegar
Salt and pepper to taste

Boil the pork until soft and tender. Reserve 2 c. of the broth. Cut pork into small cubes. Combine the broth, the pig's blood, and the cow's blood. Set aside. Saute the garlic until golden brown. Then add the onions and the tomatoes. Cook for about 10 minutes. Add the boiled pork, radish and vinegar. Cook for 5-8 minutes without stirring then add the mixture of blood broth. Season with salt and pepper and stir continuously to prevent the curdling of the blood. Cook it for 10 minutes. Serve hot or cold.

CARI-CARI DE PATA Y RABO

1 "buntot ng baka" (ox tail)
1 "pata ng baka" (ox leg)
6 c. water
½ c. atchuete seeds for
  coloring
½ c. water
4 pcs. eggplants
2 bundles sitao

1 "puso ng saging"(butuan
  variety)
1 head garlic, chopped
2 onions, sliced
¼ c. cooking oil
½ c. "bagoong alamang"
1 c. ground peanuts
1 c. toasted, ground rice

Salt and AJI-NO-MOTO

Boil the buntot and pata in water until tender. Cut into desired pieces and set aside. Soak atsuete seeds in water. Rub to bring out color. Set aside. Cut vegetables into desired pieces. Boil water, drop sitao and parboil. Remove, set aside. Do likewise with eggplants and puso ng saging. Saute garlic and onions in cooking oil. Add bagoong and atsuete water. Let boil 5 minutes. Blend in ground peanuts and ground rice. Bring to a boil then put in the meats. Just before removing from the fire, add the vegetables. Serve with Bagoong Guisado.

Bagoong Guisado

¼ c. cooking oil
1 head garlic, chopped
1 onion, chopped
¼ k. boiled pork, diced

1½ c. bagoong alamang
1 tsp. sugar
¼ c. native vinegar
¼ c. pork broth

Saute garlic and onion in cooking oil. Add the pork, bagoong and sugar. Blend well, then add vinegar and broth. Boil until quite dry. Serve with the Cari-Cari.

SWEET & SOUR KIDNEY

4 pairs pork kidney
1 tbsp. rock salt
2 stalks leeks, in 1″ pcs.
2 tbsps. cooking oil
2 tbsps. rice wine
2 tbsps. cooking oil
2 cloves garlic, crushed
¼ c. soy sauce
3 tbsps. sugar

3 tbsps. vinegar
⅓ c. water
1 tsp. Aji-no-moto
1 pc. jellyfish, (optional) diced
6 pcs. taingang daga, soaked in water
1 tbsp. cornstarch dispersed in water
Sesame oil

Half kidneys. Remove white membrane. Score outer side of kidneys. Cut into pieces. Let soak in salt 10 minutes, rinse. Cook kidneys in boiling water for 1 minute. Soak in cold water. Drain. Set aside. Saute leeks and kidneys in hot oil. Stir in rice wine, cook 1 minute more. Set aside. Brown garlic in oil. Add soy sauce, sugar, vinegar, water and Aji-no-moto. Drop the jelly fish and taingang daga. Cook 5 minutes. Thicken with cornstarch. Finally add the sauteed kidneys and flavor with sesame oil.

MENUDONG GOTO

½ k. tripe (goto)
2 tbsps. cooking oil
2 cloves garlic, crushed
1 onion. chopped
1 chorizo de bilbao or Spanish sausage, sliced

1 c. tomato sauce
1 pc. red or green pepper
1 c. cooked garbansos
2 c. broth
2 potatoes, cubed and fried
Salt to taste

1 tsp. vetsin

Clean and boil tripe in salt and water until tender. Cut into small pieces and set aside. Fry the garlic and onions in hot oil. Add the chorizo de bilbao and pour in tomato sauce. Drop in tripe, pepper, garbansos and potatoes. Simmer until sauce is of desired consistency. Just before removing from the fire, season with salt and Aji-no-moto.

112

LENGUA CON CHAMPIGNON

1 ox tongue
2 tbsps. calamansi juice
¼ c. soy sauce
¼ c. olive oil
½ c. butter
5 cloves garlic, minced
2 medium onions, chopped
⅓ c. fresh tomatoes, chopped

3 tbsps. soy sauce
Salt to taste
1 pc. bay leaf
¼ tsp. peppercorn
¼ c. white wine
Enough broth or water to
cover tongue

Rub tongue with salt and vinegar. Rinse and boil 5 minutes. Scrape white coating on surface. Marinate in calamansi juice and soy sauce 1 hour. Brown in olive oil and butter. Set aside. In the same pan, saute garlic, onions and tomatoes. Put back the tongue and blend the rest of the ingredients. Pour into large saucepan, bring to a boil, then lower heat, simmer for 3 hours or until tongue is tender. Strain sauce, set aside. Slice tongue and arrange on a platter. Prepare mushroom-butter sauce.

Mushroom-Butter Sauce

½ c. butter
½ c. mushrooms, sliced

¼ c. all-purpose flour
Strained sauce from tongue

Melt butter in skillet. Blend in flour. Add the mushrooms and strained sauce. Cook until bubbly. Water may be added if sauce is too thick. Pour over sliced meat and serve.

OX TONGUE WITH PUREED PEAS

1 ox tongue or 2 big pork tongues	¼ c. butter
1 bay leaf	2 tbsps. parsley, chopped
1 medium-sized onion	2 tsps. Aji-no-moto
Few peppercorns	¼ c. melted butter
6 cloves garlic	1 medium onion, cut into rings
1 small can anchovies	1 egg, hard cooked and sliced

Boil tongue until white coat can be scraped off easily. Boil again in fresh water with the bay leaf, onion, peppercorns and garlic. Cook tongue until soft. When cooked, transfer to a platter and cut diagonally ¾ through. Set aside. Strain anchovies to make a smooth paste. Add the softened butter blending well with parsley and Aji-no-moto. Insert mixture between slices of tongue and press together. Transfer tongue to a pyrex dish. Pour the melted butter and bake in mod. oven (350°F.) for ½ hour. Baste occasionally. Serve with Pea Sauce. Decorate with sprigs of parsley, onion rings previously fried in butter, and slices of hard-cooked eggs.

Pea Sauce

1 can green pea soup	1 tsp. Aji-no-moto
½ can water	Dash of white pepper
Salt if necessary	

Season soup with Aji-no-moto, pepper and salt (if necessary). Bring to a rolling boil stirring constantly. Boil 1 minute.

LENGUA ESTOFADA

1 ox tongue (about 1 k.)	2 fresh tomatoes, quartered
½ c. olive oil	3 stalks leeks
½ c. white wine	1 sprig parsley
¼ c. vinegar	Salt to taste
2 medium onions, quartered	2-3 c. water
1 head garlic, crushed	2 pcs. potatoes, cubed then fried in butter
12 pcs. peppercorns	
1 laurel leaf	1 c. button mushrooms, sauteed in butter
1 clove	
1 pc. carrot, quartered	Sprigs of parsley for garnishing

Rub tongue with salt and vinegar. Rinse then boil 5 minutes. Scrape white coating on the surface. Brown tongue in hot olive oil. Transfer to a large saucepan, add the rest of the ingredients except potatoes and mushrooms. Simmer gently until tongue is tender. Slice into serving pieces. Set aside. Strain sauce, put back tongue, add potatoes and mushrooms. Simmer until potatoes are cooked. Arrange on a platter, garnish with sprigs of parsley.

MEAT LOAF DE LUXE
Recipe on page 59

HOT POTATO SALAD
Recipe on page 136

LUMPIA UBOD
Recipe on page 124

ORANGE SPARE-RIBS
Recipe on page 96

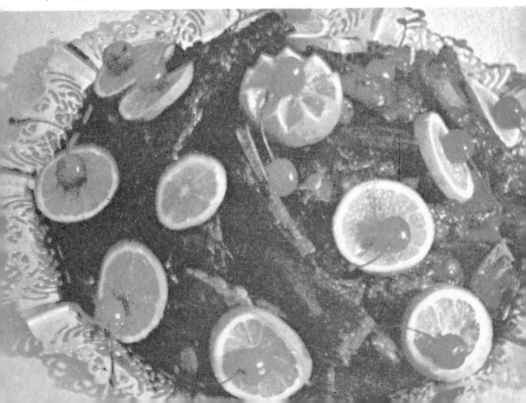

PASTEL DE LENGUA

1 pc. beef tongue	½ c. tomato sauce
½ c. cooking oil	1 tsp. salt
2 pcs. onions	2 tsp. Maggi sauce
3 pcs. carrots, cubes	2 tsps. Aji-no-moto
3 pcs. potatoes, cubes	¾ tsp. ground pepper
¾ c. green olives	1 tsp. vinegar
1 can Vienna sausage	2 c. beef tongue broth

2 — 3 tbsps. flour dissolved in
½ c. water

Boil the tongue until soft, then cut into 1″ squares. Put back into the broth and bring to a boil. Add the rest of the ingredients. Allow to simmer in the saucepan until all vegetables are cooked. Thicken sauce with dispersed flour. Let simmer for five minutes and pour into a pyrex dish. Cover with pie crust.* Brush top with beaten egg and milk. Bake until golden brown in a hot oven.

* Pie Crust:

2 c. all purpose flour	¼ c. butter
½ tsp. salt	¼ c. cooking oil

3 — 4 tbsps. cold water

Sift flour and salt together into a bowl. Blend cooking oil and butter. Cut in with pastry blender until well blended. Sprinkle water over mixture and form into a ball, press firmly. Roll out dough between 2 pieces of waxed paper. Peel off paper. Use for pastel.

Vegetables

LAKSA

¼ c. cooking oil
1 onion, chopped
½ c. shrimps, shelled and cut finely
2 eggplants cut in serving pcs.
2 c. squash, cut in serving pcs.
1 c. sigadillas, cut in ½'' pcs.
2 c. sitao, cut in ½'' pcs.

1 c. kangkong (swamp cabbage)
10 pcs. batao
1 small bundle sotanghon, soaked
¼ c. taingang daga, soaked
1 tbsp. soy sauce
1½ c. water

1 tsp. salt and Aji-no-moto

Heat cooking oil in a pan. Add onion and cook until soft. Drop the shrimps and cook for a few minutes. Add the vegetables and cover. Cook until half done. Uncover pan, season with soy sauce, salt and Aji-no-moto. Pour water, taingang daga and sotanghon. Continue cooking until done.

GULAY NA MAIZ

2 tbsps. cooking oil
3 cloves garlic, crushed
1 onion, sliced thin
¼ k. shrimps, sliced
2 c. shrimp stock

1 c. young corn, first slice
   from cob and scrape
2 tsps. patis
½ tsp. Aji-no-moto
⅛ c. pepper leaves (sili leaves)
Dash of pepper

Saute garlic. When golden brown, add onions and shrimps. Add shrimp stock and bring to a boil. Add scraped corn and simmer until the corn is cooked. Add seasonings. Add green pepper leaves and continue cooking for 3 minutes before removing from fire. Serve hot.

EGG FU YUNG

6 pcs. alimasag, boiled and
   flaked
1 tsp. minced ginger
1 tbsp. rice wine
½ tsp. salt
2 pcs. Chinese mushroom
   soaked and chopped
6 sliced bamboo shoots,
   chopped

½ stalk leek, chopped
2 tbsps. green peas
6 eggs
½ c. oil
1 c. soup stock
2 tbsps. soy sauce
1 tbsp. cornstarch, dispersed in
   2 tsps. water

Remove all meat from crab and flake; mix with ginger and wine. Beat eggs, add crab meat and salt. Heat ¼ c. oil and fry crab and egg mixture in size of a 9 inch omelet or in smaller omelets for individual servings. Fry on both sides. Heat remaining ¼ c. oil and fry mushrooms, bamboo shoots and leeks. Add soy sauce, green peas and soup stock to form sauce. When sauce boils up, thicken with cornstarch and water. Pour sauce over omelet and serve hot.

ADOBONG OKRA

20 pcs. fresh, very young okra	3 tbsps. patis
¼ c. water	4 cloves garlic, crushed
¼ c. vinegar	1 onion, chopped
½ c. pork, diced	1 tsp. pepper

Wash and parboil the okra in water. Set aside. Fry the pork. Push to one side of the pan. Saute garlic, onion and okra. Season with vinegar, patis and pepper. Cook until okra is tender crisp. (Vinegar cuts sliminess of okra.)

NOTE: Substitutes for okra may be: kangkong, sitao and puso ng saging (banana heart).

CHAYOTE MIXED PICKLES (Achara)

1½ k. chayote, cut in 1″ strips	1 sweet red pepper, the thick
2 regular sized carrots, cut in.	variety
strips	1 green pepper, the thick
20 pcs. sibuyas tagalog or	variety
shallots	1 small pc. ginger (about 2″)

Wash, peel and cut the vegetables into long thin strips. Work the vegetables individually with salt and press to remove juice. Mix all the vegetables and pack in clean dry container. Prepare the Pickle Solution:

Pickle Solution

2 c. native vinegar	1½ c. sugar
2 tsps. salt	

Boil solution. Strain and pour over the vegetables. Pack in jars. Remove air bubbles by inserting a knife around the side of the bottle. Fill up with more pickle solution. Cover tightly.

FRESH LUMPIA

3 tbsps. cooking oil	1 c. potatoes, cubed
1 tbsp. atsuete	3 c. cabbage, shredded
2 tbsps. fat	2 c. stringbeans, strips
2 cloves garlic	1 c. garbansos, cooked
½ c. onions, chopped	¼ c. kinchay, stripped
¼ k. pork, cubed	4 pcs. tokua
200 gms. shrimps shelled,	1 tsp. salt
1½ c. water	2 tbsps. patis
chopped coarsely	1 tsp. Aji-no-moto
1 c. yellow camote, cubed	20 pcs. lettuce leaves

20 pcs. lumpia wrapper *

Soak atsuete in 3 tbsps. of cooking oil.   Set aside.   Saute garlic in 2 tbsps. fat until light brown.   Add onions, pork and shrimps.   Pour in water or soup stock and cover.   Cook over medium heat until pork is tender.   Add camote, potatoes and cook for 5 minutes.   Then mix in rest of vegetables.   Strain atsuete-oil to the vegetable mixture.   Season with salt and patis.   Cook until all vegetables are done.   Add 1 tsp. Aji-no-moto.   Cool in a colander while allowing liquid to drain out. When cool, wrap in lumpia wrapper with a leaf of lettuce showing at one end.   Serve with Lumpia Sauce.**

RADISH PICKLES

1 radish	½ tsp. Aji-no-moto
3 tbsps. rock salt	½ tsp. sesame oil
2 tbsps. vinegar	3 tbsps. sugar

1 red pepper, sliced thin

Peel skin of radish thickly and slice paper thin.   Add rock salt, press down and let stand 2-3 hours or overnight.   Rinse with water until no longer salty.   Squeeze out water.   Add vinegar, Aji-no-moto, sesame oil, sugar and red pepper.

* *Recipe of Lumpia Wrapper, on page 124.*
** *Recipe of Lumpia Sauce, on page 124.*

ATSARANG SANTOL

1 dozen santol
1 c. water
1 c. native onions peeled
1 head garlic, peeled
1 c. red pepper, in strips

1 c. green pepper, in strips
Small piece ginger, in strips
1 small box raisins
3 c. native vinegar
1½ c. sugar
2 tsps. salt

Boil the santol in water 10 minutes.   Drain and cool.   Peel santol, quarter and remove seeds.   Combine santol, onions, garlic, ginger and raisins. Set aside.   In a saucepan, blend vinegar, sugar and salt. Boil.   Remove scum.   Pack vegetables in a sterilized bottle and pour boiled vinegar over.   Seal bottle immediately.   May be served after 3 days.

MONGO* GUISADO

1 c. green mongo, boiled in
3 c. water
1 tbsp. cooking oil
2 cloves garlic, crushed
1 onion, chopped
6 tomatoes, chopped
½ c. pork, boiled and sliced
  into strips

½ c. shrimps, peeled and sliced
2 tbsps. bagoong
4 c. water or broth
1 tsp. salt
1 tsp. Aji-no-moto
1 cup sitsaron or cracklings,
  cut into pieces

Boil mongo until soft.   Rub through a fine sieve or puree, set aside. Saute garlic, onion and tomatoes in oil.   Drop pork and shrimps. Cook 1 minute.   Add bagoong and mongo.   Pour water and simmer, season with salt and Aji-no-moto.   Just before taking out from the fire add cracklings.   Serve hot.

* Other vegetables may be substituted.

KALABASA WITH AMPALAYA
(5 servings)

¼ c. cooking oil
½ tbsp. garlic
¼ k. pork meat, in slices
¼ k. shrimps, sliced

1 large ampalaya fruit, cut in
   diagonal slices
2 c. kalabasa fruit (about ½ k.)
   cut into cubes
Salt or bagoong and pepper to
   taste

Saute the garlic in hot oil until golden brown. Add the pork, shrimps and the shrimp juice. Season with bagoong and pepper and cover. Cook for 15 minutes. Add kalabasa and stir. Add ampalaya (more salt may be added if needed). Cover. When vegetables are half cooked, uncover and cook till vegetables are done. Serve hot.

CHOP SUEY

2 pieces carrots, sliced
300 grams celery
½ head of cabbage
½ k. cauliflower
3 tbsp. soy sauce
1 cup chicken stock
2 tbsp. cornstarch
1 tsp. Aji-no-moto
   Salt and pepper to taste

3 tbsp. cooking oil
3 cloves garlic
1 large onion
300 grams shrimps
1 medium sized breast of
   chicken
1 c. cooked pork
½ c. chicken livers and gizzard
4 pieces chinese mushrooms
1 sweet green pepper

Cut all vegetables into serving pieces, preferably diagonally and in uniform sizes. Cut all meats and shrimps in bite size pieces and set aside. Wash chinese mushrooms and soak them in ½ cup warm water.
Saute garlic and onions in hot oil till all are golden brown. Add sliced shrimps, chicken livers and gizzards, previously cut up and the cooked pork. Season with soy sauce and salt and pepper. Pour in chicken stock. Allow to cook for about five minutes. Then add carrots, cauliflower, cabbage, chinese mushrooms with the ½ cup water it was soaked in. Allow to cook in an open pan. Add the rest of the vegetables. Cook till vegetables are almost done. DO NOT OVERCOOK! Disperse cornstarch in ¼ cup water and add to mixture. Finish with 1 tsp. of Aji-no-moto. Serve hot.

121

BURONG PAJO SALAD
(6 servings)

2 c. sliced Burong Pajo
½ tsp. salt (depending on
   saltiness of Pajo)

1 large tomato
½ c. sibuyas tagalog, sliced fine
2½ tbsps. boiled alamang
½ tsp. patis

Mix all the above ingredients in a bowl. Serve with fish paksiw or fish.

UKOY

200 gms. small shrimps	1 cake tokua or bean curd, in
2 c. togue or mongo sprouts	strips
1 c. spring onion, in strips	

Wash shrimps thoroughly, remove head leaving shells.   Prepare batter.

Batter

1 c. all-purpose flour	½ tsp. pepper
1 c. cornstarch	1 tsp. AJI-NO-MOTO
1½ tsp. baking powder	¼ c. atsuete or anatto water*
1½ tsp. salt	⅔ c. shrimps juice**
Oil for deep fat frying	1 egg, well beaten

Sift dry ingredients in a bowl.   Blend in remaining ingredients, beat thoroughly to make a smooth batter.   Set aside.   In a saucer, arrange a bed of mongo sprouts.   Garnish with spring onion and shrimps.   Add about ¼ cup batter and lower carefully into deep hot fat.   Fry until crispy on both sides.   Remove to absorbent paper.   Serve hot with vinegar-garlic sauce seasoned with salt and black pepper.
NOTE: The same recipe may be prepared using 2 cups squash, 1 cup kutsay, 200 gms. shrimps and a cake tokua or bean curd (1″ strips).

PINACBET

½-1 c. water	¼ c. bagoong (alamang)
¼ k. pork, sliced into 1″ strips	4 eggplants, quartered
⅓ c. tomatoes, chopped	2 pcs. ampalaya or amargoso,
3 cloves garlic, minced	quartered
1 tsp. chopped ginger	½ tsp. Aji-no-moto
Salt to taste	

Boil ½ - 1 cup of water in a saucepan.   Drop the pork, tomatoes, garlic, ginger and bagoong.   Simmer until pork is tender.   Add the ampalaya and eggplants and cook until done.   Season with Aji-no-moto and salt if necessary.
NOTE: Dish should have very little broth when cooked.

* *Soak 2 tbsps. anato seeds in ¼ c. warm water, strain.*
** *To obtain shrimp juice — pound the heads of shrimps, add water and strain.*

LUMPIA UBOD

2 tbsps. cooking oil	1 c. snap beans or
2 cloves garlic, crushed	habichuelas, diagonal strips
1 small onion, chopped	½ k. ubod or heart of palm, in
¼ c. cooked ham, chopped	match-like strips
¼ k. boiled pork, diced	2 c. cabbage, shredded
½ c. shrimps, chopped	2 tsps. salt
½ c. cooked garbansos or chick	24 pcs. lettuce leaves or
peas	spring onions

1 c. carrots, julienne

Brown garlic in hot cooking oil, add onions, cook slowly until soft. Add the pork, ham, shrimps and garbanzos. Simmer 5 minutes. Combine carrots, stringbeans and ubod. Cook covered until vegetables are half done. Drop the cabbage, continue cooking until done. Drain and season. Cool. Set broth aside for Brown Sauce. Wrap mixture in home-made wrapper lined with lettuce leaves or spring onions. Serve with Brown Sauce.

Home-Made Lumpia Wrapper

2 duck eggs   ½ c. cornstarch dispersed in
                               1 c. water

Separate egg yolks from egg whites. Beat egg whites until frothy. Add egg yolks and beat just to blend. Blend in dispersed cornstarch. Brush frying pan with cooking oil and heat. Spoon about 2 tbsps. batter then tilt pan to spread evenly on pan. Lift off wrapper when done.

Lumpia Sauce or Paalat

½ c. sugar	1 tsp. salt
1 tbsp. soy sauce	2 tbsp. cornstarch dispersed
2 c. broth	in ¼ c. water
	4-6 Cloves garlic, minced

Blend first 4 ingredients together. Bring to boil. Thicken with cornstarch. Sprinkle with minced garlic and serve.

AMPALAYA BRAISED WITH BEEF

½ k. ampalaya or amargoso
200 gms. beef tenderloin, sliced
   thin
2 tsps. black tausi
½ tsp. sugar

1 clove garlic, crushed
2 tsps. soy sauce
2 tbsps. rice wine
¾ c. stock
1 tsp. cornstarch

Split ampalaya.   Remove seeds and scrape white membrane.   Parboil 3 minutes, then drain.   Slice thinly, and set aside.   Wash tausi, drain, then mash together with garlic.   Heat oil in pan, add mashed tausi and stir for ½ minute.   Drop ampalaya and saute 2 minutes.   Add the beef and saute 1 minute.   Season with soy sauce, sugar and wine.   Pour in the stock.   Braise for 1 minute.   Thicken with cornstarch.   Cook and serve.

CAULIFLOWER CON CAMARRON

2 tbsps. cooking oil
2 cloves garlic, crushed
¼ k. shrimps
3 pcs. dried mushrooms,
   soaked in water
Soy sauce

Salt and Aji-no-moto
½ k. cauliflower, separated
   into flowerettes
¼ c. chicharo or pea pods
1 stalk celery, cut in 1" pcs.
1 tbsp. cornstarch dispersed in
½ c. water

Heat cooking oil in a pan.   Brown garlic.   Add shrimps and mushrooms, simmer for a while.   Season with soy sauce, salt and Aji-no-moto.   Add cauliflower, chicharo and celery.   Cook for 5 minutes. Thicken with cornstarch.

CREAM JADE

6 c. water
1 tsp. baking soda
1 k. Chinese mustard plant,
    (stems only), cut in 1"
    rectangular pcs.
2 tbsps. cream
1 tbsp. cornstarch, dispersed
    in 2 tbsps. water

3 tbsps. cooking oil
¼ c. fancy mushroom
½ tsp. salt
½ tsp. Aji-no-moto
½ c. stock
1 small pc. cooked ham,
    shredded
Few drops sesame oil

Boil water, add 1 tsp. baking soda. Drop in vegetables, boil 2-3 minutes. Drain and rinse with cold water. Mix cream and cornstarch. Saute the mustard in oil, add mushrooms, salt, Aji-no-moto and stock. Cook 2 minutes then blend cream mixture. Transfer to a platter and garnish with ham. Flavor with sesame oil.

VEGETABLES WITH CHICKEN LIVER AND GIZZARD

Chicken liver and gizzard
⅛ k. peas (chicharo)
¼ k. cauliflower
1 onion, sliced
1 pc. carrot

1 tsp. salt
2 tsps. cornstarch
¼ c. stock
1 tsp. soy sauce
¼ c. cooking oil

2 tsps. rice wine

Slice chicken gizzard and liver. Soak in a mixture of cornstarch, wine and soy sauce. Let stand 15 minutes. Fry onion and vegetables in cooking oil with 1 tsp. salt. Cook 5 minutes. Set aside. Fry gizzards until tender and then add the liver. When done put back the vegetables. Add cornstarch dispersed in stock. Finish cooking. Serve.

VEGETABLES WITH BIRD EGGS

1 c. cashew nuts	1 pc. carrot, sliced
¼ c. cooking oil	1 pc. singcamas, sliced
¼ k. shrimps	¼ k. pechay with flowers in 1″ pcs.
5 pcs. dried mushrooms, soaked in water then cut in half	1 tsp. salt
	1 tsp. Aji-no-moto
¼ k. chicharo or sweet peas	12 pcs. quail eggs, hard cooked
1 large pc. bamboo shoot, sliced	¾ c. broth
	1 tbsp. cornstarch

Fry cashew nuts. Set aside. In hot cooking oil, toss shrimps and dried mushrooms. Add chicharo, cook 2 minutes. Put in pechay stalks, rest of vegetables and lastly the leaves and flowers of the pechay. Pour in broth, continue cooking until vegetables are just done. Season with salt and Aji-no-moto. Thicken with cornstarch. Pour on a platter. Garnish with hard cooked eggs and crisp cashew nuts. Serve hot.

MUSHROOM CUPS

20 pcs. dry Chinese mushrooms (uniform size)	1 tbsp. soy sauce
	Salt, Aji-no-moto
¼ k. ground pork	1 tbsp. cornstarch dispersed in water
4 pcs. water chestnuts, chopped	½ cup stock
3 tbsps. scrapped bid-bid or other white fish*	Wansuey or Chinese celery, sesame oil

Soak mushrooms in water, remove the stems. Mix the pork, water-chesnut, scrapped bid-bid and seasonings. Fill the mushrooms with the pork mixture and steam for 15 minutes. Collect drippings. Heat the drippings and stock. Thicken with cornstarch. Pour on mushrooms. Garnish with wansuey and sprinkle with sesame oil.

* *To prepare bid-bid: Scrape meat from fish and mix with water, salt and ginger juice. Stir 10-15 minutes. See glossary for ginger juice.*

ANTIPASTO

2 medium carrots, in thin slices
1 medium cauliflower, cut
  into flowerettes
4 stalks celery, cut into
  ½" pcs.
2 pcs. red peppers, broiled
  then cut in strips

3 pcs. dill pickles, sliced
  French Dressing*
¼ c. tuna chunks
½ can spiced hot sardines,
  split
Stuffed olives and capers
  for garnishing

Blanch the carrots, cauliflower and celery separately. Drain. Marinate separately first 5 ingredients in French Dressing about 30 minutes. In a pyrex dish, arrange vegetables, tuna and sardines in layers. Pour remainder of dressing over the layers. Garnish with stuffed olives and capers. Serve cold.

ONION PIE

4 c. onions, chopped finely
½ c. butter
4 slices bacon, in pieces
¼ c. all-purpose flour

2 eggs
½ c. Carnation Evaporated Milk
⅛ tsp. pepper
¼ tsp. salt

Place onions in a deep saucepan with the butter and bacon. Cook gently for 15 minutes or until onions are very soft. Meanwhile combine flour, salt and pepper. Beat in eggs and Carnation Evaporated milk. Blend egg-milk mixture into the cooked onions. Cook 2 minutes more . Set aside. Prepare pastry for 2-crust pie.** Roll out dough. Cut to fit muffin tins. Spoon filling and bake at 400°F. until brown.

* *Recipe of French Dressing, on page 140.*
** *Recipe of pastry for 2-crust pie, on page 201.*

CABBAGE PIE

¼ k. potatoes, cooked and   1 egg yolk
    mashed   2 tbsps. butter
            ¼ c. Carnation Evaporated Milk

Cook and mash the potatoes. Add the egg yolk, butter and Carnation Evaporated Milk. Season with salt and pepper. Blend mixture well. Cover sides and bottom of a pyrex dish with Mashed Potatoes. Set aside. Prepare the Filling.

Filling

½ k. cabbage   2 tbsps. butter
2 hard cooked eggs   2 med. onions, chopped
           ¼ c. rock salt

Cut cabbage into wedges, remove core, then shred. Squeeze shredded cabbage thoroughly with ¼ cup rock salt in order to remove water. Wash and strain. Fry cabbage in a small amount of oil at high heat to allow water to escape. Add the butter and set aside. Fry onions till tender. Chop hard cooked eggs. Combine everything together. Pour this cabbage mixture on the mashed potatoes. Top with Bechamelle Sauce. Sprinkle with cheese, and bake at 350°F. until delicately brown.

Bechamel Sauce

2 tbsps. butter   2 tbsps. flour
1 c. milk   ½ c. grated cheese (for
   Salt and pepper   topping)

Melt the butter and add the flour. Add milk slowly and cook stirring continuously until thick. Season with salt and pepper.

CABBAGE ROLL

1 head cabbage, (about ½ kilo)	1½ tsps. salt
¼ k. beef, ground	¼ tsp. pepper
¼ k. pork, ground	¼ tsp. oregano
1 onion, minced	½ c. rice (raw) optional
	1 c. tomato sauce or 1 c. fresh tomatoes, chopped

Boil cabbage for 5 minutes.   Remove from water and separate leaves. Mix remaining ingredients together, except tomatoes.   Stuff leaves with filling and roll. Fasten with toothpick.   Arrange in a saucepan. Pour tomatoes, cover and simmer about 1½ hours.

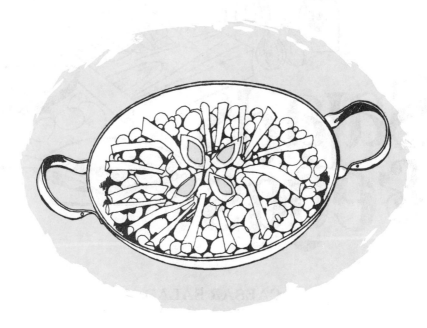

MENESTRA DE VERDURAS

2 tbsps. lard or pork fat
1 c. bacon or ham, strips
½ k. potatoes, diced
½ k. onions, chopped
¼ k. Baguio pechay, cut in
    serving pcs. and blanched
¼ k. cauliflower, in flowerettes,
    blanched

½ c. flour
1 tbsp. flour
2 c. soup stock
    Salt to taste
1 tsp. Aji-no-moto
½ c. green peas
8 pcs. asparagus
1 hard cooked egg, sliced

Fry bacon in pork fat. Push to one side of the pan. Add potatoes and onions, cook until done, set aside, with the bacon. Dredge pechay and cauliflower in flour. Fry, set aside. In the fat where all of these ingredients have been fried, blend in flour and brown. Add stock. Season with salt and Aji-no-moto. Put back everything in the pan. Cook over slow flame until done. Add green peas and asparagus. Garnish with hard cooked eggs. Serve hot as a first course.

Salads & eggs

CAESAR SALAD

1 large head lettuce, torn to bite-size pcs.	½ c. bacon, in thin strips
4 pcs. salad tomatoes, in wedges	1 c. bread cubes
	¼ c. grated cheese
	Dressing

Chill lettuce and tomatoes separately.   Fry bacon until crisp, set aside. Brown bread cubes in bacon fat.   Set aside.   Just before serving, toss ingredients together leaving some croutons, tomatoes and cheese for garnishing.

Dressing

1 egg	½ tsp. salt
½ c. olive oil or salad oil	1 tsp. worcestershire sauce
¼ c. lemon juice	1 tsp. sugar
1 clove garlic, mashed	1 tbsp. anchovy
½ tsp. pepper	fillet, mashed

Beat eggs slightly.   Blend in rest of ingredients.   Pour in a glass jar, cover and shake.   Chill.   Just before using, reshake to blend.

STUFFED EGGS

6 hard cooked eggs
½ tsp. salt
¼ tsp. white pepper
½ tsp. Aji-no-moto
½ tsp. prepared mustard
1 tbsp. chopped onions
2 tbsps. chopped pickles
Mayonnaise to moisten egg
    mixture

Native lettuce or head
    lettuce
6 large tomatoes
½ tsp. paprika
Sliced cucumber
Sprigs of parsley

Slice pointed tops of eggs. Make short diagonal cuts around edge of white to produce zigzag effect. Set aside. Mash yolks, blend in seasonings, onion, pickles and enough mayonnaise to moisten. Fill egg whites with mixture. Chill. Slice tops of tomatoes. Scoop out seeds. Arrange the tomatoes on a lettuce bed. Nestle a stuffed egg on a tomato and pipe mayonnaise with a pastry tube. Sprinkle with paprika. Garnish with cucumber slices and sprigs of parsley.

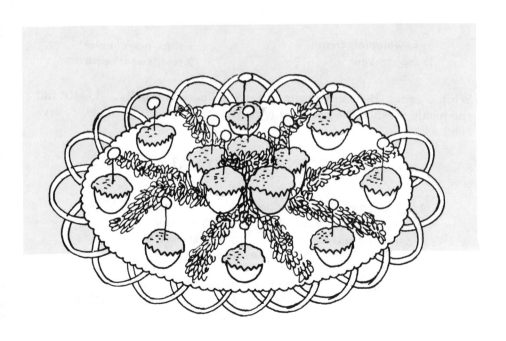

PICKLED EGGS

1 doz. quail or hen's egg,
hard cooked

Pickling Solution

1 c. vinegar
½ c. brown sugar

1 tsp. allspice, wrapped in
cheesecloth

1 tsp. salt

Combine all ingredients together and boil 10 minutes. Drop eggs and simmer 5 minutes. Set aside. Prepare vegetables.

Vegetables

1 medium carrot, cut fancily
1 slice green papaya,
shredded

1 green pepper, cut in long
thin strips
1 tsp. salt

Combine ingredients together. Let stand 5 minutes. Rinse with hot water. Add to eggs in pickling solution. Pack in sterilized jars and seal. Pickles will be ready 2-3 days after preparation. Drain and chill. Prepare sauce.

Sauce

½ c. whipping cream
½ tsp. vinegar

1 tbsp. mayonnaise*
2 tsps. sweet relish

Whip cream. Beat in vinegar and mayonnaise gradually. Lastly add the pickle relish. Fold pickled eggs and vegetables into sauce. Serve cold.

CHICKEN POTATO SALAD

1 c. cooked chicken, shredded
2 c. cooked potatoes, cubed
½ c. cooked carrot, cubed

¼ c. celery, cut in ¼" pcs.
2 tbsps. sweet relish
¼ c. cooked beets, diced

1 c. mayonnaise*

Combine all ingredients except beets together. Blend thoroughly. Fold in beets. Serve cold on a bed of lettuce. Garnish with chopped eggs and parsley.

* Recipe of Mayonnaise, on page 141.

CHEF'S SALAD

1 large head lettuce, torn into bite-size pcs.
1 cucumber, sliced
3 salad tomatoes, in wedges
1 c. celery, cut into ½" pcs.
½ c. cooked beef or pork tongue, in strips

½ c. cooked ham, in strips
½ c. swiss or cheddar cheese, in strips
½ c. cooked chicken meat, shredded
2 hard cooked eggs, sliced

Chill vegetables separately. Prepare French Dressing.* Chill. Arrange meats and cheese on top of vegetables in salad bowl. Just before serving, add French dressing, toss all ingredients together. Serves 10.

COLESLAW

1 medium cabbage, (about 2 c.) shredded
1 carrot, shredded

½ c. raisins
½ c. pineapple tidbits, drained
¼ c. peanuts, chopped

½ - ¾ c. Mayonnaise**

Toss ingredients together. Add mayonnaise and blend well. Serve cold.

* *Recipe of French Dressing, on page 140.*
** *Recipe of Mayonnaise, on page 141.*

HOT POTATO SALAD

6 slices bacon, cut into pieces
4 pcs. hot dog, sliced
4 c. raw yellow potatoes,
   cubed (about ¾ k.)
½ c. onions, chopped

1 c. boiling water
1 tall can Carnation
   Evaporated Milk
2 tsps. prepared mustard
½ c. vinegar
1 tsp. salt

¼ tsp. white pepper

Cook bacon. Set aside. Fry hot dogs in bacon fat. Set aside. Fry onions and potatoes. When fat is absorbed, add water, then Carnation Evaporated Milk. Continue cooking over low heat stirring occasionally until potatoes are cooked and sauce thickens. Mix vinegar, salt, mustard and pepper. Add this to potato mixture very slowly stirring constantly. Do not allow sauce to dry. Remove from fire, add fried bacon and sliced hot dog. Serve hot. Serves 6.

GREEN SALAD

1 medium head lettuce, torn
   into bite-size pcs.
4 pcs. tomatoes, cubed

½ pc. Baguio cucumber, in
   ½" pcs.
3 stalks celery

French Dressing*

Prepare vegetables and chill separately. Toss together lightly with French Dressing.*

* Recipe of French Dressing, on page 140.

136

SUMMER VEGETABLE SALAD

1 cup boiled potatoes, in cubes
1 cup cucumber, peeled, seeded, in cubes
1 cup stringbeans, boiled, cut diagonally

1 pc. green pepper, in strips
2 big red firm tomatoes, cut in cubes
¼ k. shredded cabbage

Chill above ingredients.   Before serving, add Tomato French dressing and serve immediately.

TOMATO FRENCH DRESSING

A very good dressing, passed on to me by Alita. Very practical. Can be kept for weeks in the refrigerator.

½ c. sugar
2 tsp. salt
1 tsp. mustard
¼ tsp. paprika

1 can tomato soup
1 onion, finely chopped
¾ c. vinegar
1¼ c. salad oil

Place all ingredients in a wide wide mouthed bottle. Shake throughly until all ingredients are thoroughly blended. Chill. Store in refrigerator. Serve with salads.

ROYAL RUSSIAN SALAD

2 c. cooked potatoes, cubed
1 c. cooked carrots, diced
1 c. cooked stringbeans, in
 ¼″ pcs.
1 c. sweet peas, drained
1 c. sweet mixed pickles

1 c. cooked chicken, shredded
1 - 2 c. mayonnaise*
1 c. cooked beets, diced
1 hard cooked egg, sliced
 Few leaves head lettuce
 Sprigs of parsley

In a bowl, toss lightly first 6 ingredients together.   Moisten with mayonnaise.   Put in beets and toss with more mayonnaise.   Mold salad and serve cold on a bed of crisp lettuce.   Garnish with hard cooked egg slices and sprigs of parsley.

PINEAPPLE-BUCO SALAD

1 can Liberty Condensada
2 egg yolks
 Meat or 2 buco (young
 coconut)

1 can pineapple tid-bits
1 c. kaong or sugar palm,
 boiled until tender

Cook Liberty Condensada and egg yolks over double boiler until thick. Stir continuously. Cool. Blend buco, pineapple, kaong and salad dressing. Pour into a pan and chill. Serve cold.

* Recipe of Mayonnaise, on page 141.

PAMPANGO FROZEN FRUIT SALAD

2 c. fruit cocktail
1 c. Queen Anne cherries
1 c. peaches, in 1" cubes
1 c. pineapple chunks
1 c. fresh apples, in 1" cubes,
   marinated in juice or syrup
   to prevent discoloration

1 c. lacatan banana slices,
   marinated in juice or syrup
¼ k. grapes, peeled
Orange sections
Chopped almonds
1 c. whipping cream, whipped
   stiff

½-1 c. mayonnaise*

Chill all fruits, dipped in syrup or juice to prevent discoloration or drying out. When cold, drain all fruits. Be careful to keep each piece of fruit intact. Set aside. Fold in whipped cream into mayonnaise. Carefully fold whipped mixture into fruits. Arrange fruit salad in a bowl and garnish with maraschino cherries. Fruit Salad may be served as is. Or, freeze, and then serve. Serves 12.

Recipe of Mayonnaise, on page 141.

FRENCH DRESSING

1 c. salad oil
⅓ c. vinegar
1 tsp. mustard

1 dash of freshly ground pepper
Salt to taste

Place salt and mustard in a bowl and beat in vinegar thus allowing salt
to dissolve.   Add oil gradually and season with pepper.
Or, place all ingredients in a covered jar and shake vigorously.   Store
in refrigerator and use just before serving salad.

MAYONNAISE

1 egg yolk	⅛ tsp. pepper
½ tsp. salt	1½ tbsps. vinegar or
1 tsp. sugar (optional)	1½ tbsps. calamansi or lemon juice
¼ tsp. mustard	1 c. salad oil or cooking oil

Combine all ingredients except the salad oil in 1 qt. bowl. Beat thoroughly. Add salad oil, one tsp. at a time beating well after each addition. After all the salad oil has been added, beat one more minute or until mayonnaise is thick enough to hold its shape when spooned out. Makes about 1¼ cup mayonnaise.

rice noodles & pastas

ARROZ CALDO WITH GOTO

½ kilo goto or tripe, boiled till tender
3 cloves garlic, minced
1 onion, chopped
2 tbsps. patis (fish sauce)
1½ c. rice, washed

6 c. broth from goto
6 cloves, garlic
3 tbsps. cooking oil
2 stalks spring onion
2 calamansi
Patis

Pepper

Clean the tripe well and boil in water, until tender. Cut tripe into serving pieces. Saute garlic in cooking oil until golden brown. Set garlic aside. Saute onion in the same fat. Add patis and washed rice. Pour broth and boil. Stir occasionally until it looks like porridge. Add tripe and season to taste. Top with fried garlic, spring onions, and pepper. Serve hot with calamansi and patis.

MAYA TAMALES

1 pkg. Maya Bibingka Mix
2 c. rich coconut milk and
2 c. diluted coconut milk from
  2 coconuts
1 med.-sized onion, minced
3 tbsps. cooking oil
1-3 tsps. black pepper
½ tsp. salt
4 tbsps. peanut butter or ½ c.

finely chopped peanuts
Banana leaves, wilted over
  fire, cut into 3″ strips
½ c. ham, cut into strips
½ c. bacon, cut into strips
½ c. chicken, cooked, cut into
  strips
3 hard cooked eggs, sliced
½ c. cooked shrimps (optional)

Blend Maya Bibingka Mix and 2 cups diluted coconut milk until smooth. Saute onion in cooking oil until soft but not brown. Add bibingka-coconut milk mixture to onions. Cook, stirring constantly to prevent lumping. Add black pepper and salt. Continue cooking until thick. Gradually add thick coconut milk and stir well until smooth and thick. Remove from fire. Put ¼ portion of the cooked mixture in a separate bowl and add the peanut butter or chopped peanuts. Blend well. Arrange two strips of banana leaves crosswise. In center of cross lay a tablespoon of the white mixture and top with a tsp. of the peanut mixture. Arrange strips of ham, bacon, chicken or pork, a slice of egg and shrimps. Pat in the form of a square. Wrap with banana leaves and tie securely or use aluminum foil for the outer wrapping; taking care to seal openings securely. Drop tamales in briskly boiling water (enough to cover all) and boil in tightly covered pan for half an hour. Remove at once from water to prevent a soggy tamales. Cool before unwrapping and serving. Makes 20 tamales.

PANCIT LUGLOG
Red Sauce

½ c. cooking oil
6 cloves garlic, minced
1 c. cooked pork, diced
2 cakes tokua or bean curd, diced

¼ c. atsuwete water (2 tbsps. anato seeds soaked in ¼ c. water)
1 c. shrimp juice
½ c. kintsay or Chinese celery

Salt and pepper to taste
1 tsp. Aji-no-moto

Brown garlic in hot oil. Set aside for garnishing. Drop pork in cooking oil, fry until slightly brown. Add tokua and fry 1 minute. Add the concentrated atsuwete water. Pour the 1 cup concentrated shrimp juice and bring to a boil. Add the kintsay and season with salt, pepper and Aji-no-moto. Set aside.

Palabok

2 c. shrimp juice
¼ c. atsuwete water, (2 tbsps. anato seeds soaked in ¼ c. water)

6 tbsps. flour dissolved in ½ c. water
1 tsp. Aji-no-moto
Salt to taste

Soak atsuwete seeds in water, rub, to bring out color and strain. Add this to shrimp juice and put the mixture in a saucepan. Disperse flour and add to mixture. Bring to a boil while stirring constantly. Season with salt and Aji-no-moto. This is the sauce for the pancit which is called "palabok".

Pancit

2 qts. water
½ k. dried rice noodles, (bijon) soaked in cold water for 10 minutes then drained

1 c. mongo sprouts, (bean sprouts) without the long tail, boiled

Garnishing

½ c. flaked smoked fish (tinapa)
½ c. crisp cracklings or bacon rind (sitsaron), pounded
2 hard cooked eggs, chopped

½ c. fresh shelled, boiled shrimps
½ c. finely sliced green onions
6 pcs. calamansi or 1 lemon, in slices

Patis

Measure 2 qts. water into a deep container and bring to a boil. Put a handful of togue into a sifter then add the bijon. Dip sifter into boiling water for 1 minute, then drain well. Continue until all the bijon has been cooked in boiling water. Pour noodles into a large platter. Cover with palabok. Top palabok with the pork and tokua mixture. Sprinkle finely flaked tinapa, sitsaron, chopped eggs and shelled shrimps. Sprinkle with chopped green onion, fried garlic, salt and pepper. Season with calamansi and patis.

SOTANGJON

¼ c. cooking oil
½ head garlic, crushed
1 onion, sliced
1 stewing chicken, quartered
10 c. water
1 carrot
2 stalks leeks
2 stalks celery

1 tsp. salt
1 tsp. Aji-no-moto
2 tbsps. patis
1 c. taingang daga;* soaked
10 pcs. dried mushrooms,
    soaked in water & sliced
200 gms. sotangjon, soaked in
water for 10 minutes

Saute the garlic and onion in hot oil. Add the pieces of chicken and cook 5 minutes. Pour water and add the vegetables. Let boil. When chicken is tender, remove from broth and flake the meat. Strain broth. Press vegetables then asieve to get all the flavor. Season with salt, Aji-no-moto and patis. Pour back chicken meat, add taingang daga, mushroom and sotangjon. Boil 10 minutes. Serve hot with Biscocho.

* *See glossary.*

CHOW MEIN

8 pcs. dried mushrooms,
soaked, then sliced
¼ c. cooking oil
4 cloves garlic, crushed
2 onions, sliced
1 c. lean pork, thinly sliced
8 pcs. ham, sliced
1 chicken, broiled
20 pcs. shrimps
½ tsp. salt

½ c. celery, diced
½ c. leeks, in ½" pcs.
2 tbsps. cornstarch
2-½ c. chicken stock
¼ c. soy sauce
2 tbsps. Aji-no-moto
½ tsp. salt
¼ tsp. pepper
1 pkg. pancit canton

Fry mushroom in hot oil. Push to one side of pan. Saute garlic and onions. Add pork and chicken. Simmer covered for 5 minutes. Add ham and shrimps, simmer 2 minutes. Add vegetables, salt and cook 5 minutes more. Disperse cornstarch in chicken stock season with soy sauce, Aji-no-moto, salt and pepper. Add to meat and vegetable mixture. Cook until thick. Set aside. Fry noodles in hot cooking oil till crisp. Arrange on a platter. Spoon topping. Serve.

FRIED MILK

2 c. cooking oil
100 gms. bijon — rice sticks
8 egg whites
2 egg yolks

½ tsp. salt
1 tsp. Aji-no-moto
1 c. crab meat
1 c. cream

Wansuey (Chinese parsley)

Heat oil until extremely hot. Drop bijon, fry until puffed. Arrange in a platter. Beat eggs slightly, season with salt and Aji-no-moto. Saute crabmeat in 3 tbsps. fat. Lower flame. Stir in the cream. Add slightly beaten eggs. Stir till mixture thickens slightly. Pour over fried bijon. Decorate with wansuey. If desired, sprinkle with sesame oil. Serve at once.

CHINESE FRIED RICE

4 strips bacon, cut finely
2 eggs, slightly beaten
2 c. cooked rice
¼ c. pork, boiled
1 tbsp. soy sauce

¼ c. cooked ham
¼ c. shrimps
1 tbsps. green onion, cut fine
2 tsps. Aji-no-moto
Salt and pepper to taste

Fry bacon until slightly brown. Remove bacon from skillet and fry the beaten eggs in bacon fat. Set some aside. Add cooked rice and fry for 5 minutes. Mix thoroughly. Add all other ingredients, cooked bacon and seasonings. Garnish with scrambled eggs, ham and green onion.

SIO MAI

Wrapper

1 c. water
1 tbsp. lard

¼ tsp. salt
1½ c. all-purpose flour

Combine water, lard and salt. Boil. At boiling point, pour in flour. Beat until it forms a ball. Put the dough on slab. Divide into 1½″ balls. Roll the dough till paper thin. Set aside.

Filling

1 c. shrimps, chopped
¼ c. ground pork
1 c. singcamas, chopped
¼ c. spring onion, chopped
1 onion, chopped
1 egg
1 tsp. soy sauce

⅛ tsp. pepper
½ tsp. Aji-no-moto
1 tsp. salt
Sio Mai wrapper
Salad oil or cooking oil
Calamansi or lemon juice
and soy sauce

Combine first 10 ingredients in a mixing bowl. Wrap about 1 tbsp. of mixture in a sio mai wrapper. Shape each in a bonnet-like poach. Brush with salad oil. Arrange in a steamer and steam for 30 minutes. Serve with soy sauce and calamansi or lemon juice.

PANCIT BIJON GUISADO

¼ c. cooking oil
2 cloves garlic, minced
1 onion, minced
1 c. boiled pork, sliced
1 small cabbage, shredded
1 large carrot, strips
2 tbsps. soy sauce
1½ c. broth

1 bunch kintsay or Chinese leeks
1 bundle 1st class bijon China (rice sticks)
1 tsp. salt
1 tsp. Aji-no-moto
2 pcs. chorizo canton, (Chinese sausage) fried and sliced
Spring onion, chopped

Saute garlic in cooking oil, add onions, pork, carrot and cabbage. Season with soy sauce and fry for 2 minutes. Add broth and simmer, add kinchay. When vegetables are cooked, mix in soaked and drained bijon and season with salt and Aji-no-moto. Garnish with chorizo canton and spring onions. Serve with calamansi.

PANCIT CANTON

¼ k. shrimps
1 tbsp. cornstarch
1 eggwhite
1 chicken breast
1 tbsp. cornstarch
1 eggwhite
2 cloves garlic, crushed
1 onion, chopped
¼ k. lean pork, sliced
5 pcs. chicken liver
2 tsps. salt
1 tsp. Aji-no-moto

2 tbsps. soy sauce
1½ c. broth
1 carrot, in strips
1 head cauliflower, cut into
   flowerettes
4 cabbage leaves, shredded
¼ c. chicharo or pea pod
⅓ c. kutsay
2 tbsps. cornstach, dispersed
   in ¼ c. water
1 pkg. pancit canton (Dried
   Chinese noodles)

Peel shrimps leaving tail. Devein. Coat with cornstarch and egg white. Set aside. Slice chicken breast, coat with cornstarch. Saute garlic, onion, pork, chicken liver, shrimps and chicken meat. Season with salt, Aji-no-moto and soy sauce. Pour broth and bring to a boil. Add all the vegetables. Thicken with dispersed cornstarch. Stir canton and cook 10 minutes. Serve hot.

SPECIAL CHINESE RICE PORRIDGE
LUGAO MACAO SPECIAL

1 c. rice
10 c. broth
3 pcs. kangiocho
¼ k. shrimps, chopped
½ k. ground pork
5 pcs. waterchestnuts,
   chopped
¼ c. spring onion, chopped

4 big pcs. mushrooms, cut in
   strips
2 eggs
1 tbsps. cornstarch
2 tsps. salt
1 tsp. Aji-no-moto
¼ k. pork liver, thinly sliced
   Bitchu-bitchu (shrimp fritter)*

Cook rice in water or in broth with kangiocho. Mix the shrimps, pork, water chestnuts, spring onions, mushrooms, eggs, cornstarch, salt and Aji-no-moto together in a bowl. Form into ½″ balls. Set aside. When rice is almost cooked drop in the bola-bola one at a time, put in the thinly-sliced liver. Season with salt and Aji-no-moto. Mix the lugao mixture constantly (5 minutes) to have a nice stock. Serve in bowl with 1 raw egg (optional) and the bitchu-bitchu.

* Bitchu-bitchu can be obtained in Chinese market.

149

ARROZ A LA PAELLA

20-25 pcs. clams
2 pcs. crabs (alimasag)
300 gms. medium-sized shrimps
1 chicken (about 500 gms.), cut up
⅛ c. olive oil
¼ k. pork, cut in serving pcs.
1·50 gms. ham, cut in 1" squares
1 pc. chorizo de bilbao, sliced
4 cloves garlic, crushed
1 medium onion, chopped fine

1 c. tomato sauce
1½ c. rice, washed
3½ c. broth
1 pc. red pepper, in strips
10 pcs. string beans
2 tsps. salt
1 tsp. Aji-no-moto
¼ c. peas
2 hard cooked eggs
1 sprig parsley
Slices of lemon

Boil clams, set aside 1 cup broth.   Boil crabs and shrimps together.
Set aside.   Boil bony parts of the chicken.   Set broth aside.   Heat olive
oil in a steel or a heavy pan or paellera.   Fry chicken, pork, ham and
chorizo.   Cover until half done.   Push to one side.   Saute garlic,
onion and tomato sauce.   Add clam and chicken broth and rice.   Mix
everything together.   When rice is half way done drop the red pepper,
string beans, clams.   Season with salt and Aji-no-moto.   Cover tightly
and allow to cook without stirring for 20 minutes or until all the broth
is absorbed by the rice.   Paella may be baked in the oven.   (Keep pan
covered).   During the last 5 minutes of cooking put shrimps, crabs
and peas on top.   Garnish with sliced eggs, strips of pepper and parsley
and lemon slices.

CANELLONI A LA TOSCANA
Pasta

1⅓ c. all-purpose flour   1 egg
¼ tsp. salt   1 egg yolk

Measure flour and salt in a bowl. Break in eggs. Knead to a smooth dough. Roll out dough very thin. Cut into 3½" squares. Drop squares in salted boiling water. Cook 1 minute or until tender but firm. Plunge in cold water and dry with a towel. Set aside. Prepare the Tomato Sauce, White Sauce and filling.

Tomato Sauce

2 c. tomato sauce   Salt and pepper to taste
1 tsp. garlic, macerated   ¼ c. butter
1 c. broth   Aji-no-moto

Melt butter in a saucepan. Stir in tomato sauce, garlic, broth, salt and pepper. Lastly, add the Aji-no-moto. Stir over the fire until it boils then simmer for a few minutes.

White Sauce

½ c. butter   ¼ tsp. pepper
½ c. flour   2 c. Carnation Evaporated Milk
½ tsp. salt   2 c. water

Melt butter. Blend in flour and seasonings. Pour in Carnation Evaporated Milk and water. Cook until bubbly. Set aside. Prepare Filling.

Filling

3 tbsps. butter   1½ c. cooked chicken, ground
1 clove garlic, crushed   ¼ c. cooked ham, ground
1 onion, chopped   ¼ tsp. thyme
8 pcs. chicken liver or   ½ tsp. salt
½ c. liver paste   ¼ tsp. pepper
1 pc. pork brain   1 tsp. Aji-no-moto

2 eggs
½-1 grated cheese

Melt butter in a pan. Saute the garlic, onions, liver and brain. Grind sauteed mixture with chicken and ham. Season with thyme, salt, pepper and Aji-no-moto. Break in the eggs. Blend mixture thoroughly. Put about a tbsp. of mixture on each square of pasta and roll. Arrange cannelone side by side in a shallow baking dish. Cover with white sauce and tomato sauce. Make more layers if desired. Sprinkle generously with grated cheese. Broil.

CARBONARA

200 gms. bacon, cut in fine pcs.
1 head garlic, crushed
⅓ c. Baguio green pepper, (sweet variety), diced
⅓ c. red pepper (sweet variety) or pimientos, diced
1 8-oz. pkg. spaghetti
2 eggs, well beaten
2 tbsps. Carnation Evaporated Milk
½ tsp. salt
½ c. grated cheese

Fry bacon. Set aside. In 2 tbsps. bacon fat, brown garlic lightly. Add green and red pepper. Set aside. Cook spaghetti. Drain. While hot, fold in beaten eggs, Carnation Evaporated Milk, salt, some bacon, sauteed peppers and cheese. Garnish with rest of bacon, sauteed peppers and cheese. Serve at once.

SOPA SECA ITALIANA

1 chicken (about 500 gms.) (cooked)
1 box macaroni
3 tbsps. margarine
6 strips bacon, cut in pieces
1 pc. chorizo de bilbao, sliced
5 cloves garlic, crushed
1 onion, chopped
⅓ c. tomatoes, chopped
1 c. tomato sauce
Salt and pepper to taste
¾ c. grated cheese

Flake chicken meat. Set aside. Boil macaroni in chicken stock until just tender. Set aside. Heat margarine in a pan. Fry bacon and chorizo de bilbao. Set aside. In same pan, saute garlic, onion and tomatoes. Add tomato sauce. Simmer 2 minutes. Add the chicken, bacon and chorizo de bilbao. Simmer 2 minutes. Remove pan from fire. Blend in ½ cup grated cheese and macaroni. Pour in a pyrex dish, sprinkle remaining cheese. Broil until done.

LASAGNA
Pasta Verde

3 c. spinach leaves   3 c. all-purpose flour, sifted

3 eggs

Boil spinach in 1 cup water. Squeeze out water. Chop or grind spinach to make into paste. Set aside. Make a well in mound of flour on a board. Break in eggs one at a time, mixing lightly after each addition. Add spinach. Knead well to make a stiff and smooth dough. Divide. Flour may be added if necessary to make a stiff dough. Roll out each half to about ⅛″ thick and cut into 4″ x 4″ pieces. Prepare Tomato Meat Sauce.

Tomato Meat Sauce

¼ c. olive oil	¼ tsp. nutmeg
½ c. butter	¼ tsp. oregano
2 clove garlic, crushed	1 tsp. salt
⅔ c. onion, chopped	½ tsp. pepper
½ k. beef round, ground	1-2 c. beef broth or hot
200 gms. ground pork	water
4-6 tbsps. white wine	1 c. tomato sauce
2 bay leaf	

Heat olive oil and butter. Brown the garlic, add the onions, cook gently until soft. Put in the ground beef, ground pork, wine and spices. Allow to cook for a while then pour in ahe beef broth and tomato sauce. Simmer gently for 1 hour or until thick. Set aside. A little flour may be added to thicken the sauce. Prepare the Bechamel Sauce.

Bechamel Sauce

1 c. butter	3 c. evaporated milk
⅔ c. flour	2 tsp. salt
3 c. hot water	½ tsp. pepper
2 c. grated cheese	

Melt butter in a pan. Blend in flour. Gradually stir in the hot water and evaporated milk. Cook until bubbly. Season with salt and pepper. Set aside. Boil 6 cups water with 2 tbsps. olive oil and 1 tsp. salt. Drop in pasta verde (about 6 pcs. at a time). Bring back water to a rolling boil, before dropping more pasta. Plunge pasta in cold water. Dry on a towel. Grease a pyrex dish with butter. Pour about ⅓ of the Bechamel Sauce. Arrange a layer of pasta. Spoon in tomato meat sauce, and sprinkle generously with cheese. Repeat. Bake at 350°F. until top is golden brown. Let stand about 5-10 minutes to set layers. Serve.

RAVIOLI
Dough

1½ c. all-purpose flour
2 egg yolks

¼ tsp. salt
¼ c. lukewarm water

Measure 1½ cups flour on a board. Make a well and drop egg yolks.
Add salt and lukewarm water. Knead thoroughly until slightly elastic.
Put in a bowl, and let stand 10 minutes. Roll out dough thinly. Spoon
a heaping tbsp. of filling about 2″ apart on one half of the rolled dough.
Cover with other half dough, moisten area around each filling, press
sheets together around each mound of filling. Run a pastry wheel
around the mounds to cut into 2″ x 4″ pieces. Drop into simmering
chicken broth or salted water. Cook 10 minutes or until tender. Remove to a towel. Arrange ravioli in a platter. Sprinkle with cheese.
Spoon tomato sauce. Serve with more cheese and tomato sauce.

Filling

2 tbsps. olive oil or cooking
oil
1 clove garlic, crushed
½ c. ground beef
½ c. ground pork

½ c. salami, chopped
2 eggs
2 tbsps. parsley, chopped
⅓ c. grated cheese
Salt and pepper to taste

1 tsp. Aji-no-moto

Heat olive oil. Brown the garlic. Add the ground beef, pork and salami. Cook 2 minutes. Remove from fire and cool mixture slightly.
Blend in eggs, parsley and cheese. Season with salt, pepper and Aji--
no-moto.

Tomato Sauce

2 cloves garlic, crushed
1 onion, chopped
2 tbsps. butter

½ c. tomato paste
1½ c. broth or hot water
1 tsp. Aji-no-moto

¼ tsp. salt

Saute garlic, onions and tomato paste in butter. Pour in broth. Simmer until thick. Strain. Season with Aji-no-moto and salt.

PIZZA PIE

2½ tsps. yeast	1 c. boiling water
2 tbsps. lukewarm water	1 tsp. sugar
2 tbsps. lard or vegetable fat	1½ tsp. salt
3 - 3½ cups all purpose flour	

Soak yeast in lukewarm water. Dissolve lard, sugar and salt in hot water. Cool to lukewarm. Add yeast and half of the flour. Beat until smooth and soft dough is formed. Add rest of flour. Knead and smoothen into a ball. Let rise in a bowl covered for at least 1 hour or until double in bulk. Roll out directly on an ungreased cookie sheet. Brush with salad oil or cooking oil and spread with topping. Bake at 400°F. for about 35 minutes. Cut and serve at once.

Topping

1 medium onion, minced	½ tsp. oregano
1 clove garlic, chopped	½ tsp. worcestershire sauce
1 tbsp. cooking oil	½ tsp. white pepper
1 6 oz. can tomato paste	½ tsp. salt
¾ c. water	Dash of Tobasco or Red Devil

Saute onion, garlic in oil until light brown. Add tomato paste. Mix in water, stir well to blend. Add oregano, worcestershire sauce, salt, pepper and dash of tabasco. Stir mixture. Cover and simmer for sometime. Spread the following on dough with tomato paste mixture: ½ cup grated cheese, 10 round slices native cheese (kesong puti) or Mozzarella cheese, 1 small can tuna or ½ of big size can, 1 medium sweet green pepper (sliced into strips), ½ cup boiled peeled shrimps (about ⅛ kilo), 6 pcs. half-fried longanisa macao or Italian sausage.

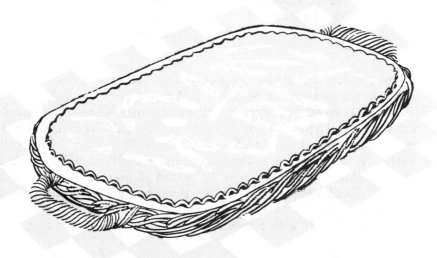

SPARERIBS & EGG NOODLE CASSEROLE

6 c. water	1 c. tomato sauce
4 pcs. bouillon cubes	1 tbsp. parsley, chopped
⅓ c. olive oil	1 tsp. pimenton
1 k. pork spareribs, cut in serving pcs.	2 tsps. Aji-no-moto
4 pcs. pork sausage, sliced	1 pkg. egg noodles (about 200 gms.
1 head garlic, crushed	2 tsps. salt
⅔ c. onion, chopped	¼ tsp. pepper
	⅔ c. grated cheese

Boil water, drop bouillon cubes, stir to dissolve. Set aside. Heat olive oil. Brown spareribs. Set aside. Drop in pork sausage, fry. Set aside. In same oil, saute garlic, onion and tomato sauce. Add parsley, pimenton and Aji-no-moto. Put back spareribs and pork sausage in pan, let simmer 2 minutes. Pour sparerib mixture into bouillon water. Bring to a boil, lower heat, simmer until spareribs are almost tender. (More hot water may be added if necessary). Put in egg noodles. Add 3 cups boiling water, cover pan and cook until noodles are tender. Season with salt and pepper. Transfer to a pyrex dish, sprinkle generously with cheese. Broil. Serve hot.

Cakes

COCONUT-PILI CHOCOLATE CAKE

Follow the Basic Chocolate Cake recipe.*   Cover top with Coconut-Pili Frosting.

Coconut-Pili Frosting

1 can Carnation Evaporated Milk	1 tsp. vanilla
3 egg yolks	1⅓ c. fresh coconut**
½ lb. butter	1 c. chopped pili nuts

Combine first 4 ingredients together.   Cook and stir over double boiler until mixture thickens.   Add coconut and pili nuts.   Beat until frosting is thick enough to spread.

* *Recipe of Basic Chocolate Cake, on page 166.*
** *To prepare coconut: Grate coarsely 1 young coconut. Bake 10 minutes at 200°F. to dry partially.*

NO-BAKE FRUIT CAKE

1 c. Liberty Condensada
2 tsps. grated lemon rind
2 tbsps. lemon juice
2-3 c. marshmallows, cut in
  small pieces with scissors
1 pkg. (7¼ oz.) pitted dates
  cut in pcs. with wet scissors

1 jar (8 oz.) candied fruits
4½ c. Graham cracker crumbs
2 c. nut meats, coarsely
  chopped maraschino or
  candied cherries

Crush graham crackers crumbs and sift through a coarse sifter. Set aside. Combine Liberty Condensada, lemon rind and juice, marshmallow, dates, candied fruits, nuts and graham crackers in a bowl. Blend until fruits and nuts are well coated with graham crackers crumbs. Pack mixture firmly into a 9 inch loaf pan lined with waxed paper. Cover with tin foil and store in a cool place at least two days before serving. Remove cake from pan, peel off waxed paper and decorate with candies cherries. Slice and serve.

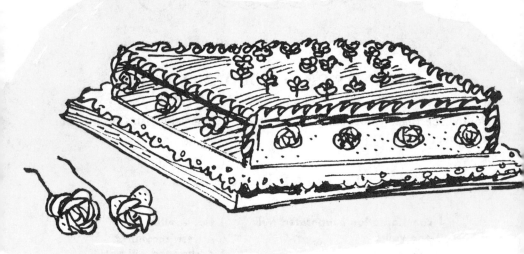

SUGAR FLOWERS

2 egg whites
3 c. powdered sugar

Juice of 1 calamansi

Beat egg whites slightly. Add powdered sugar gradually beating well after addition. Add calamansi juice. Mix well. Add desired food coloring. If sugar gets too stiff to work with, add a few drops of calamansi.

VIRGINIA OCAMPO CHEESE CHIFFON CAKE
(Prize winning cake)

2 c. White King cake flour	¾ c. water
¼ c. cornstarch	1 tsp. dayap rind
1 c. sugar	1 c. cheese, finely grated
1 tsp. baking powder	(queso de bola)
1 tsp. salt	8 egg whites
½ c. cooking oil	½ tsp. cream of tartar
7 egg yolks	½ c. sugar

Preheat oven at 325°F. Measure and sift into a bowl flour, cornstarch, 1 c. sugar, baking powder and salt. Make a well in the center of the dry ingredients. Pour the cooking oil, egg yolks, water and dayap rind. Blend thoroughly. Fold in grated cheese. In a big bowl, beat the egg whites and cream of tartar until frothy. Add the half cup of sugar and continue beating until stiff peaks are formed. Gradually fold the egg yolk mixture into the beaten egg whites. Pour into a 10″ x 4″ tube pan. Bake at 325°F. for 55 minutes. Increase to 350°F. and bake until done (about 10 minutes).

Butter Cheese Icing:

1 c. butter	¾-1 c. Carnation Evaporated Milk
¾-1 c. sugar	1 c. grated cheese

Cream the butter. Gradually add the sugar and beat after each addition. Add the Carnation Evaporated Milk gradually and beat until smooth. Separate approximately ¾ c. of the icing. To this, add ½ c. grated cheese. Paint cheese-butter icing over and around the cake. Broil for 3-5 minutes. Cool. Spread remaining butter icing on cake and sprinkle with rest of cheese. Serve.

BANQUET LAYER CAKE

3 c. cake flour, sifted
3½ tsps. baking powder
1 tsp. salt
¾ c. butter or margarine
1½ c. sugar
1⅓ c. Carnation Evaporated Milk

1 tsp. vanilla
1 tsp. almond extract
7 egg whites
½ c. sugar
3 pcs. 9 inch layer pans or
13" x 9" rectangular pan

Sift dry ingredients together. Cream butter and add sugar gradually. Combine Carnation Evaporated Milk, vanilla and almond extract, add alternately with the dry ingredients to creamed mixture. Blend well after each addition. Set aside. Beat egg whites until stiff but not dry, add sugar gradually. Beat until stiff. Fold into batter. Pour into prepared pan. Bake at 350°F. for 30 to 40 minutes. Cool and frost with De Luxe White Frosting.*

DE LUXE WHITE FROSTING

1 recipe White Mountain
  Frosting*
½ c. chopped walnuts or
  almonds

¼ c. maraschino cherries.
  drained & cut finely
½ c. chopped dates or raisins

Add chopped fruits and nuts to White Mountain Frosting and spread between and on Banquet Layer Cake.

* Recipe of White Mountain Frosting on page 158.

SPEEDY CARAMEL FROSTING

¼ c. butter or margarine
½ c. brown sugar, firmly packed
¼ c. Carnation Evaporated Milk

1½ c. confectioner sugar
⅓ c. cashew nuts, chopped
½ tsp. vanilla

Melt butter in saucepan. Add brown sugar and cook over medium heat for 2 minutes, stirring constantly. Add Carnation Evaporated Milk, continue stirring and bring to a boil. Remove from heat. Blend in confectioners sugar and chopped nuts and mix well. Add vanilla, beating until of spreading consistency.

CAKE FROM BLUMS, SAN FRANCISCO

2½ cup cake flour
1 cup sugar
3 tsps. baking powder
½ cup melted butter
5 egg yolks

¾ cup water
1 cup egg whites
½ tsp, cream of tartar
½ cup sugar
1 tsp. vanilla

Sift flour, sugar, baking powder, salt into mixing bowl. Make a "well" then add melted butter, egg yolks, water and vanilla. Beat with spoon until smooth. In a large bowl beat egg whites and cream of tartar until soft peaks form. Add sugar gradually until stiff peaks form. Pour egg yolk mixture in a thin stream over egg whites, gently cutting and folding with rubber scraper. Fold gently, bringing scraper across bottom of bowl and continue folding until completely blended. Bake in a 10" tube pan at 325° F. for 55 minutes, then at 350°F. for 10-15 minutes or until surface springs back when lightly touched. Invert pan immediately and let cool. Cut cake from tube pan across to make two layers. Frost and fill with butter cream icing.

Butter-Cream Icing:

1 c. sugar
1 c. fresh milk

1½ c. butter
1 c. whipping cream

Dissolve sugar in milk. Set aside. Cream butter until light and fluffy. Beat whipping cream until fluffy, do not over-beat. Fold into butter icing.

Caramel Crunch:

2 pcs. egg whites
2 c. brown sugar

1 tsp. baking soda
1 tsp. salt

1 c. water

Dissolve brown sugar in water. Add salt and baking soda. Bring to a boil and let cook till sugar caramelizes. (Before sugar begins to get bitter). Beat egg whites till stiff but not dry. Pour brown sugar syrup over the beaten eggs making a brown meringue. Spread meringue on a tray and bake in a slow oven (250°F. until meringue is brown and completely dry). Allow to cool. Scrape off pan. Meringue will be in bite sized pieces. Store in dry tightly covered bottle. To serve, sprinkle on top of iced cake and serve at once. Meringue should be crunchy.

(This is a cake which had been flown all the way from San Francisco, USA. I may not have been able to duplicate the cake exactly but the results are quite pleasing.)

BUTTER CAKE

3¼ c. cake flour	4 eggs, separated
4½ tsps. baking powder	¾ c. Carnation Evaporated Milk
1¼ c. sugar	½ c. water
¾ c. butter	¼ tsp. cream of tartar
	1½ tsps. vanilla

Sift flour and measure. Sift flour and baking powder together. Cream the butter. Add sugar gradually. Continue beating until mixture is light and fluffy. Frequently scrape the sides of the bowl. Drop egg yolks into the mixture one at a time beating well after each addition. Add the dry ingredients and Carnation Evaporated Milk alternately, beginning and ending with flour. Beat egg whites and cream of tartar until very stiff. Fold into butter-flour mixture. Pour into lined (ungreased) rectangular pan. Bake at 350°F for 30 to 40 minutes or until golden brown. Frost with desired icing.

BROWN SUGAR CHOCOLATE FROSTING

½ c. brown sugar	2 c. confectioner sugar
½ c. water	⅛ tsp. salt
2 tbsps. butter or margarine	¼ c. Carnation Evaporated Milk
2 squares (2 oz.) unsweetened chocolate	1 tsp. vanilla

Combine sugar, water and butter in a saucepan. Cook to soft ball stage (236°F.). Remove from heat. Add unsweetened chocolate, stir until melted. Blend in confectioner's sugar and salt alternately with the Carnation Evaporated Milk beating well. Add vanilla.

DEEP SOUTH CARAMEL CAKE

3 c. sifted all purpose flour	⅓ c. shortening
3½ tsp. baking powder	4 eggs, unbeaten
1 tsp. salt	1¼ c. water
2 c. sugar	1 tsp. vanilla

Sift dry ingredients together and set aside. Add sugar gradually to shortening, creaming thoroughly. Add alternately with the dry ingredients to creamed mixture. Blend well after each addition. Pour into three well greased and lightly floured 9" layer pan. Bake at 360°F. for 25 to 30 minutes. Cool. Frost with Hasty Butterscotch Frosting.*

Hasty Butterscotch Frosting:

⅔ c. butter	⅓ c. Carnation Evaporated Milk
1½ c. brown sugar (well packed)	4 to 4½ c. sifted confectioner sugar
	1 tsp. vanilla

Melt butter in saucepan over low heat. Blend in brown sugar, boil over low heat for 2 minutes stirring constantly. Stir in Carnation Evaporated Milk, cook until mixture comes to a boil, gradually add confectioner sugar and vanilla. Beat until of spreading consistency.

QUICK BUTTER FROSTING

¼ c. soft butter	¼ tsp. salt
1 lb. or 3½ c. sifted powdered sugar	4-5 tbsp. Carnation Evaporated Milk
	1 tsp. vanilla

Cream butter and add one cup powdered sugar gradually. Add salt and 2 tbsp. Carnation Evaporated Milk. Add remaining sugar and Carnation Evaporated Milk until a good spreading consistency is obtained. Add vanilla.

PINEAPPLE-UPSIDE DOWN CAKE

2 tbsps. butter
½ c. brown sugar
4 slices pineapple, drained
¼ c. pineapple juice
1¼ c. cake flour
2 tsp. baking powder

½ tsp. salt
⅓ c. butter
½ c. sugar
1 pc. egg, unbeaten
½ c. milk
½ tsp. vanilla

Melt butter in 8 x 8 inch pan.   Sprinkle with sugar and pour pineapple juice. Arrange pineapple slices. Sift dry ingredients together.Set aside. Cream butter and add sugar gradually, creaming well.   Add unbeaten egg and beat well.   Combine milk and vanilla.   Add alternately with dry ingredients to creamed mixture.   Blend well after each addition. Pour over pineapple. Bake on moderate oven 375°F. 45 minutes. Let stand 5 minutes, turn upside down.

MOCHA ROLL

1 c. sifted cake flour
1 tsp. baking powder
¼ tsp. salt

3 eggs
1 c. sugar
⅓ c. water

1 tsp. vanilla

Grease a 15-½" x 10-½" jelly roll pan and line with brown paper or with aluminum foil.   Sift together first three ingredients.   Set aside.   Beat the eggs in a bowl until very thick and lemon-colored. Gradually beat in sugar. Blend ⅓ c. water and vanilla. Slowly mix in dry ingredients to egg mixture just until batter is smooth.   Pour into prepared pan. Bake at 375°F. for 12 to 15 minutes or until top springs back when lightly touched. Loosen edges and immediately turn upside down on a towel sprinkled with sugar. Carefully remove paper. Trim off any stiff edges (scissors are easiest for this). While cake is still hot, roll cake in towel sprinkled with sugar. Cool. Unroll again. Spread Mocha filling, roll. Cut into 1-inch slices.

Mocha Filling:

½ lb. butter
2 c. powdered sugar

3 tbsps. strong coffee
½ c. cashew nuts, coarsely
chopped

Cream butter until light and fluffy. Add sugar alternately with the milk and coffee mixture.   Blend well.   Add chopped cashew nuts.

SUGAR AND SPICE CAKE

¼ c. sugar
2 tsp. cinnamon
3 tbsps. water
1¾ c. all purpose flour
2 tsp. baking powder

½ tsp. salt
⅓ c. butter
1 c. sugar
⅛ c. Carnation Evaporated Milk
1 tsp. vanilla

2 egg whites

Combine sugar, cinnamon and water in sauce pan. Cook, stirring constantly, until mixture begins to boil. Remove from heat, set aside. Sift dry ingredients together. Cream butter and add sugar gradually. Combine Carnation Evaporated Milk and vanilla. Add alternately with the dry ingredients to creamed mixture. Blend well after each addition. Beat egg whites until stiff but not dry. Fold into batter. Pour into well-greased and lightly floured 9 x 9 x 2 inch pan. Drizzle cinnamon syrup over top, cut back and forth through batter with knife for marble effect. Bake at 350°F. 35 to 40 minutes.

BASIC CHOCOLATE CAKE

1 c. butter
1½ c. sugar
5 egg yolks
⅔ c. cocoa

2½ c. cake flour
1 tsp. baking soda
1 c. Carnation Evaporated Milk
  with 1 tsp. vinegar
5 egg whites   or calamansi
½ c. sugar

Cream butter until light and fluffy adding the sugar and yolks gradually. Sift flour, soda and cocoa together. Add the flour-cocoa-soda mixture alternately with the Carnation Evaporated Milk beginning and ending with the flour mixture. Beat egg whites adding the sugar gradually until stiff but not dry. Fold the egg whites into the chocolate mixture using the cut and fold strokes. Pour into prepared pans and bake in moderate oven (350°F.) for 40-45 minutes or until cake springs back when lightly touched. Cool the cake.

MACAPUNO CHIFFON CAKE

1 ¾ c. all purpose flour, sifted
¼ c. cornstarch
4 tsps. baking powder
1 tsp. salt
½ c. granulated sugar
½ c. cooking oil
7 egg yolks
½ c. water

½ c. macapuno syrup
2 tbsps. pineapple juice
1 tsp. vanilla
1 c. egg whites
½ tsp. cream of tartar
½ c. granulated sugar
½ c. grated sweetened macapuno, drained and chopped

Pre-heat oven to 325°F. Sift first 5 ingredients into a mixing bowl. Make a well in center and add in next 6 ingredients. Blend well until smooth. Beat egg whites with cream of tartar until soft peaks are formed. Add sugar gradually and continue beating until very stiff. Fold in egg yolk mixture into beaten egg whites until blended. Fold in well drained, chopped sweetened macapuno. Pour into ungreased 10-inch tube pan. Bake at 325°F for 50 minutes, then at 350°F for 10 minutes. Invert pan over neck of bottle to cool. Loosen with spatula to remove. Frost with white icing.* For more flavor, slice cake into 2 layers and fill with macapuno before frosting.

* *Recipe for White Icing, on page 176.*

Sweetened Macapuno:

1 c. granulated sugar
1 c. water
½ c. grated macapuno

¼ tsp. anis, wrapped in a
piece of cloth

Boil sugar and water. Add macapuno and anis, continue simmering until macapuno is nearly transparent and syrup has become slightly thick. Strain and cool. Remove anis. Spread macapuno on clean board and cut into small bits.

BLITZ TORTE

½ c. butter or margarine
½ c. sugar
4 egg yolks
1 tsp. vanilla
2 c. sifted cake flour
1 tsp. baking powder

3 tbsps. Carnation Evaporated Milk
4 egg whites
¾ c. sugar
¼ tsp. cinnamon
½ c. chopped cashew or
walnuts

Pre-heat oven to 350°F. Line bottom and sides of 2-8" layer cake pans, extend paper beyond sides of pan. Cream butter until light. Gradually add the sugar and egg yolks beating well after each addition. Blend in vanilla. Sift flour and baking powder together. Beat in flour-baking powder mixture with Carnation Evaporated Milk beginning and ending with flour mixture. Pour into prepared pans. Set aside. Beat 4 eggwhites. Add sugar and beat until stiff peaks are formed. Pile onto batter. Sprinkle with cinnamon and cashew nuts. Bake at 350°F. for 15 minutes. Prepare ½ recipe of cream filling.* Spread cream filling between two layers. Serve.

DARK FRUIT CAKE

2 c. raisins
1 c. dates, chopped
2 c. candied fruits
1 c. pili, chopped coarsely
1½ c. all-purpose flour
¼ tsp. baking soda
¼ c. honey or light molasses

½ tsp. cinnamon
¾ tsp. all-spice
½ c. butter
½ c. sugar
3 eggs, unbeaten
¼ c. rum or brandy

Heat oven to 275°F. Grease and line a tube pan or a loaf pan with wax or brown paper. Put raisins, dates, glazed fruits and pili nuts in a bowl. Sift flour, baking soda, cinnamon and all-spice over fruits. Toss fruits until well coated with flour. Set aside. In a large bowl, cream butter, add the sugar and eggs gradually, beating well after each addition. Stir in fruit-flour mixture alternately with brandy and molasses. Spoon into prepared pan and bake 3½ hours. Cool. Wrap in aluminum foil and store in tight container to keep well. If desired, moisten with rum or brandy occasionally.

* *Recipe of Cream Filling, on page 203.*

PILI CREAM CAKE

1 c. caramelized pili nuts,* chopped	1 c. sugar
2 c. all purpose flour	1 egg
2½ tsps. baking powder	2 egg yolks
½ tsp. salt	1 c. Carnation Evaporated Milk
½ c. butter or margarine	1 tsp. vanilla

Sift dry ingredients together. Cream butter adding sugar gradually, creaming well. Add unbeaten egg and egg yolks. Combine Carnation Evaporated Milk and vanilla. Add alternately with the dry ingredients to creamed mixture. Blend well after each addition. Fold in chopped pili nuts, reserving 1/4 cup. Turn into two 8" round layer pans, well greased and lightly floured. Bake at 350°F. for 30 to 35 minutes. Cool. Spread cream filling between layers.**

Meringue:

3 egg whites	¼ tsp. cream of tartar
¼ tsp. salt	6 tbsps. sugar

Combine and beat first 3 ingredients together until slight mounds form. Add sugar gradually beating well after each addition. Continue beating until meringue stands in stiff glossy peaks. Cover top and sides with meringue. Sprinkle with reserved nuts. Brown at 350°F. for 12-15 minutes.

  * Caramelized pili nuts can be bought in bottles.
** Recipe of cream filling on page 203.

CHOCOLATE BEEHIVES

Prepare Basic Chocolate Cake.*   Cut into 2″ x 2″ square pieces.   Top with graduated mounds of White Mountain Frosting.**   Cover with Chocolate Sauce.

Chocolate Sauce

2 squares or 2 oz. chocolate   2 lbs. powdered sugar
2 tbsps. butter   ⅓ c. Carnation Evaporated Milk
¾ c. corn syrup

Combine all the ingredients on top of a double boiler.   Cook stirring constantly until thick.

* Recipe of Basic Chocolate Cake, on page 166.
** Recipe of White Mountain Frosting, on page 176.

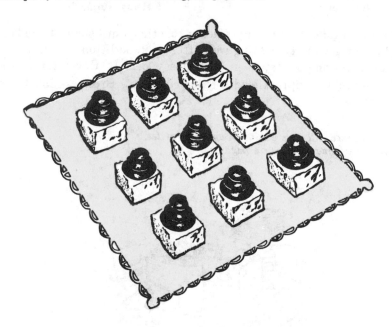

170

PRUNE CAKE

½ c. Carnation Evaporated Milk	1 c. sugar
¼ c. water	4 egg yolks
1 tsp. calamansi or	2½ c. sifted cake flour
lemon juice	1 tsp. baking soda
1 c. prunes	1 tsp. baking powder
¼ c. water	4 egg whites
1 butter or margarine	½ c. sugar

Combine Carnation Evaporated Milk, water and calamansi juice. Let stand until milk coagulates. Boil prunes in water until soft. Pit, then chop. Set aside. Cream butter until light and fluffy. Gardually add sugar and egg yolks beating well after each addition. Sift flour, soda and baking powder together. Beat flour mixture alternately with sour milk. Blend in prunes. Set aside. Beat egg whites until soft peaks are formed. Gradually add sugar, beat until stiff but not dry. Fold into prune mixture. Pour into a paper-lined 13" rectangular pan and bake at 350°F. for 35-40 minutes or until done. Cool and split cake. Fill cut layer with Prune Butter Icing. Replace top and frost sides and top with Prune Butter Icing.

Prune Butter Icing

Prepare Butter Icing,* set aside ¼ cup, add ⅔ cup chopped prunes to remaining icing.   Use to fill and frost cake.   Decorate with remaining ¼ c. butter icing

* *Recipe of Butter Icing, on page 176.*

BASIC SPONGE CAKE

1 c. sifted cake flour	2 tbsps. cold water
1 tsp. baking powder	1 tsp. vanilla
¼ tsp. salt	½ c. sugar
5 egg yolks	5 egg whites
¼ tsp. salt	½ c. sugar

Sift flour, baking powder and salt together. Set aside. Beat egg yolks with salt, cold water and vanilla until light. Gradually add sugar, beating well until thick and lemon-colored. Set aside. Beat egg whites until soft peaks are formed. Gradually add sugar, beating well until very stiff but not dry. Fold egg yolks alternately with flour-mixture into egg whites. Pour into prepared pans. Bake at 350°F. about 20-25 minutes. Cool and frost with favorite icing.

MACAPUNO ROLL

Follow Sponge Cake recipe.*   Pour into a paper-lined jelly roll pan.
Bake at 350°F. for 20-25 minutes or until done.   Invert immediately on
a towel dusted with powdered sugar.   Roll.   Cool.   Unroll and fill
with Macapuno Filling.   If desired frost with White Mountain Frosting.

Filling

4 egg yolks or 2 eggs   1 can Liberty Condensada
¼ c. all-purpose flour
¼ c. butter or margarine   1 c. macapuno, grated
                    1 tsp. vanilla

Blend first 4 ingredients together.   Cook over double boiler until thick.
Add macapuno and cook 2 minutes more.   Add vanilla.   Cool.

* *Recipe of Basic Sponge Cake, on page 172.*

MOCHA CAKE

5 eggs	¾ c. plus 2 tbsps. cake flour,	¼ c. melted butter, cooled
¾ c. sugar	sifted 3 times	

Beat eggs until fluffy. Add the sugar gradually and beat until thick. Fold in flour and melted butter. Pour in a 13" x 9" x 2" paper-lined pan. Bake at 325°F. 20 minutes. Invert at once on a cake rack and cool completely. Split cake and sprinkle with 1 tbsp. creme de cacao. Fill and frost with Mocha Icing.

Mocha Icing

3 egg yolks	¾ c. Carnation Evaporated Milk	1½ tbsps. instant coffee
½ c. sugar	3 tbsps. creme de cacao	¾ c. butter

Beat egg yolks slightly. Blend sugar and Carnation Evaporated Milk. Cook over low fire, stirring constantly till mixture coats the spoon. Cool. Cream butter and add cooled egg yolk mixture gradually. Blend in creme de cacao and instant coffee.

NOTE: If you wish to tint icing for decoration, remove enough icing before adding coffee infusion.

MANGO CAKE

10 egg whites	10 egg yolks	1 tsp. vanilla
1 c. sugar	¼ c. water	1 c. sugar
	2 c. sifted cake flour	

Beat egg whites until foamy. Gradually add sugar, continue beating until very stiff but not dry. Set aside. Beat egg yolks with water and vanilla until creamy. Gradually add sugar, beating well until thick and lemon colored. Fold egg yolks alternately with flour into egg whites. Pour in a paper-lined 13" x 9" rectangular pan and bake at 350°F. 20-25 minutes. Cool. Prepare Icing.

Icing

1 c. sugar	1 c. whipped cream (chilled)
1 c. fresh Carnation Evaporated Milk	4 ripe firm mangoes, peeled and sliced into 1" x 2½" pcs.
1½ c. butter	

Dissolve sugar in Carnation Evaporated Milk, set aside. Cream butter until light and fluffy. Beat in milk mixture until smooth. Blend in whipped cream. Set aside. Split cake. Spread icing on cut layer, arrange sliced mangoes, leaving several pieces for topping. Place other half of cake on top and ice all around. Garnish with sliced mangoes. Chill and serve.

174

MOCHA PRALINE ROLL

Prepare sponge cake.* Pour into a paper-lined jelly roll pan and bake at 350°F. 20-25 minutes or until done. Invert immediately on a towel dusted with sugar. Roll. Cool. Fill with Mocha Praline. Frost with Mocha Icing.

Mocha Icing

Prepare Butter Icing** and add 1 tbsp. instant coffee. Set aside 1 c. for frosting, use ¾ c. for Mocha Praline.

Mocha Praline

½ c. sugar
1 tbsp. butter

¼ c. chopped cashew or
    walnuts

¾ c. Mocha Icing

Caramelize sugar. Add butter and nuts. Cook 2 minutes more. Pour into a greased pan or board. Cool. Crush with a rolling pin. Blend into Mocha Icing.

* *Recipe of Sponge Cake, on page 172.*
** *Recipe of Butter Icing, on page 176.*

WHITE MOUNTAIN FROSTING

¾ c. sugar
3 tbsps. water
⅓ c. corn syrup or

¼ tsp. cream of tartar
3 egg whites
1 tbsp. vanilla

Mix sugar, water and corn syrup in a saucepan. Bring to a boil. Remove cover and cook until syrup spins a 6-8″ thread. Just before syrup is ready, beat egg whites until stiff enough to hold to a point. Pour hot syrup gradually in a thin stream into the beaten egg whites Continue to beat until frosting holds peaks. Blend in vanilla. Makes 1½ c. frosting.

BUTTER ICING

¾ c. sugar
1 c. butter
¾ c. Carnation Evaporated Milk

Dissolve sugar in Carnation Evaporated Milk. Set aside. Cream butter until light and fluffy. Pour sugar-milk mixture in thin streams beating continuously until well blended.

NOTE: To shorten creaming time use 1 cup powdered sugar instead of granulated sugar.

ORANGE CHIFFON CAKE

2½ c. cake flour	5 egg yolks
1 c. sugar	¾ c. orange juice
3 tsps. baking powder	1 c. egg white
1 tsp. salt	½ tsp. cream of tartar
½ c. cooking oil	½ c. sugar

1 tsp. orange rind

Sift flour, sugar, baking powder, salt into mixing bowl. Make a "well", then add in order: cooking oil, egg yolks, orange juice and orange rind. Beat with spoon until smooth. In a large bowl, beat egg whites and cream of tartar until they form very stiff peaks. Add ¼ cup sugar. Do not underbeat. (a dry rubber scraper drawn through whites leaves a clean path). Pour egg yolk mixture in a thin stream over egg whites, gently cutting and folding with rubber scraper. Fold gently, bringing scraper across bottom of bowl and continue folding until completely blended. Bake in a 10" tube pan at 325°F. for 55 minutes, then at 350°F. for 10 to 15 minutes or until surface springs back when lightly touched. Invert pan immediately on funnel. Let hang until cold. To remove, loosen with spatula. Turn pan over and hit edge sharply on table. Frost as desired.

VARIATIONS: ¾ cup of any fruit juice or any flavored liquid (pineapple juice or coffee) desired, may be substituted for the ¾ cup orange juice. Omit rind.

LECHE FLAN

2 c. Carnation Evaporated Milk	1 tsp. lemon rind or vanilla
8 egg yolks	1 c. sugar
½ c. caramel syrup*	

Scald the Carnation Evaporated Milk in double-boiler 15 minutes. Beat egg yolks. Add the sugar, milk and flavoring. Pour into 1 quart mold. Place this in large pan half-filled with water. Steam or bake for about 1 hour or until mixture becomes firm. Cool before removing from mold. (If desired, line mold with the caramel syrup before pouring in mixture for steaming or baking).

* *Recipe of Caramel Syrup, on page 183.*

PUTO

¼ c. shortening
3 tbsps. sugar
1 c. flour
1 tsp. baking powder

⅛ tsp. salt
6 tbsps. Carnation Evaporated
Milk
4 egg whites
2 tbsps. sugar

Cream shortening and add 3 tbsps. sugar. Sift dry ingredients together and add alternatively with 6 tbsps. Carnation Evaporated Milk (this is a little over 1/3 c. milk). Set aside. Beat egg whites until stiff. Add 2 tbsps. sugar (this helps keep the air in the beaten eggwhites). Fold the eggwhites and pour into muffin. Steam for about 20 minutes or until done. Serve hot or cold.

Note: A few anis seeds sprinkled on puto adds to flavor.

NENA ZAFRA'S CASSAVA BIBINGKA

7 c. grated cassava
3 whole eggs
2½ c. sugar
1 tall can Carnation Evaporated
Milk

2 tall cans coconut milk (using
the Carnation Evaporated Milk
can for measuring)
¼ c. melted margarine

Mix all the ingredients together. Blend well. Put in muffin pans and bake at 350°F. for 30 to 35 minutes or until done.

Topping:

1 can Carnation Evaporated Milk
1 c. thick coconut milk
2 egg yolks, slightly beaten

2 tbsps. sugar
2 tbsps. flour

Put the first four ingredients in a saucepan and boil, stirring constantly. When thick, add the slightly beaten egg yolks. Cook for 2 minutes. Spread on top the cooked cassava and broil at 400°F for 10 minutes or until golden brown.

ALMOND JELLY WITH CHERRIES

1 bar white gulaman or agar   ¼ c. Carnation Evaporated Milk
2 c. water   ½ c. sugar
              ½ tsp. almond flavor

Boil gulaman in water until dissolved. Add Carnation Evaporated Milk
sugar and almond flavor. Strain into molds and allow to set.

Syrup

½ c. sugar   Ice cubes
¼ c. water   ¼ tsp. almond flavor

Combine ingredients for syrup. Chill. Cut gulaman into squares,
transfer into serving bowl, add syrup. Garnish with maraschino
cherries.

CORNELL FUDGE

⅓ c. cocoa   1 tsp. light corn syrup
¾ c. Carnation Evaporated Milk 3 tbsps. butter
2 c. sugar   1 tsp. vanilla
              1 c. nuts (optional)

Melt chocolate in Carnation Evaporated Milk. Add sugar and corn syrup.
cook slowly, stirring until sugar is dissolved. Cook gently to soft ball
stage* stirring frequently. Remove from heat. Add butter and cool at
room temperature to lukewarm without stirring. Add vanilla. Beat
vigorously until fudge becomes very thick and loses its gloss. Quickly
spread in greased pan. When firm cut in squares. One cup broken nuts
may be added. Or fudge may be kneaded when hard, formed into rolls
and sliced.

* A soft ball should be formed when a tsp. of mixture is dropped into cup of cold water.

BRAZO MERCEDES
Filling

1 c. Liberty Condensada
1 tsp. vanilla

8 egg yolks
2 tbsps. butter

Combine eggyolks and Liberty Condensada. Cook on top of a double boiler. Continue cooking until thick or of spreading consistency. Add the butter and vanilla. Blend well. Set aside.

Meringue

8 egg whites
1 tsp. cream of tartar

1 c. sugar
1 tsp. vanilla

Beat eggwhites and cream of tartar until it stands in peaks. Add the 1 cup of sugar gradually, beating continuously. Flavor with vanilla. Spread meringue onto a heavily oiled brown paper-lined cookie sheet or force meringue through a cake decorator or cookie tube. Bake at 400°F. until brown. Loosen paper lining. While hot, spread the above filling. Roll as for jelly roll.

HOLIDAY PUDDING

½ loaf bread
2 cans Carnation Evaporated Milk
2 eggs, slightly beaten
½ c. raisins

½ c. glazed fruits
½ c. sugar
½ c. caramelized sugar for bottom of pan

¼ c. water

Dissolve sugar in Carnation Evaporated Milk. Remove all crust from bread and soak in milk mixture for 20 minutes. Add eggs, raisins and glazed fruits. Blend very well. Coat bottom of a loaf pan with caramelized sugar. Pour in pudding mixture. Bake in a pan of water in a 350°F. oven, until knife comes out clean. About 40 minutes. Cool. Invert on platter. Serve.

* Recipe of Caramel Syrup, on page 183.

MARUYA

1 c. sifted all-purpose flour
1 tsp. baking powder
1 tsp. salt
2 eggs
½ c. Carnation Evaporated Milk

1 tsp. melted fat or
vegetable lard
Saba bananas, sliced
lengthwise

Sift dry ingredients into a bowl. Set aside. Mix eggs Carnation Evaporated Milk and oil. Add to dry ingredients. Beat until smooth. Dip saba in batter and deep-fat fry. Drain on absorbent paper. Roll in sugar.

Variation: Sweet camote (sliced thinly) may be used instead of saba bananas.

MERINGUE TORTE

6 egg whites
1 tsp. vanilla

½ tsp. vinegar
1½ c. sugar

Line the bottom of 2 8″ round pans with brown or wax paper. Beat egg whites until they form soft peaks. Blend in vanilla and vinegar. Gradually add sugar beating well till very stiff. Spread meringue in prepared pans and spread evenly to edges. Bake in slow oven (300°F.) 1½ hours or until dry on top and lightly brown. Cool thoroughly in pans. Turn out and peel paper. Prepare Mocha Filling.

Mocha Filling

2 sq. chocolate, melted
1 tbsp. instant coffee,
dissolve in
¼ c. water
2 eggs

1 c. butter
2 c. sugar
½ c. cashew nuts or walnuts,
chopped

Combine chocolate, coffee infusion and eggs. Cool. Cream butter until light. Gradually add sugar and chocolate-egg mixture, beating well after each addition. Fill layers. Frost top and sides. Sprinkle nuts Chill overnight.

CANONIGO

8 egg whites
½ c. sugar

1 tsp. baking powder
1 c. caramelized sugar*
2 tbsps. butter

Line 2 loaf pans or desired mold, with caramelized sugar. Rub with butter. Set aside. Beat eggwhites until soft peaks form. Gradually add sugar and baking powder, beating continuously until eggwhites are very stiff. Pour meringue in prepared molds, place in pans half-filled with water and bake at 350°F. for 30 minutes or until brown. Cool and unmold in a platter. Prepare the sauce.

Sauce

½ c. sugar
8 egg yolks
1 tsp. vanilla

1 c. Carnation Evaporated Milk
¼ c. rhum

Combine first 3 ingredients together. Cook over double boiler until thick. Remove from fire and add vanilla and rhum. Cool. Spoon over canonigo or serve separate.

Caramelized Sugar*

1 c. sugar

½ c. hot water

Melt sugar in heavy metal container. As soon as sugar is golden brown, add ½ cup hot water to dissolve caramelized sugar and form syrup. May be stored in covered bottle.

UBE JAM

2 c. ube, or yams, boiled, mashed

1 c. sugar
2 c. Carnation Evaporated Milk

Combine Carnation Evaporated Milk, ube and sugar. Cook over a low flame until thick. Keep on stirring to prevent scorching.

SANS RIVAL

6 egg whites	**1½ c. cashew nuts, chopped**
¾ c. sugar	**finely**
	1 tsp. vanilla

Grease and flour heavily 3 inverted 18″ x 15″ cookie sheets. Set aside. Beat egg whites until soft peaks are formed. Gradually add the sugar, beating well after each addition. Continue beating until egg whites are very stiff. Fold in cashew nuts and vanilla. Spread thinly in prepared pans. Bake at 300°F. for 20 minutes or until golden brown. Cut wafers in the center if desired. Loosen and slide wafers to a flat surface. Cool. (Work while wafers are hot because they are hard to loosen as they are crisp when cool.) Prepare filling .

Filling

1 c. sugar	**6 egg yolks**
⅓ c. water	**½ lb. butter**
	2 tbsps. rum

Boil sugar and water until it spins a thread. Meanwhile, beat egg yolks until thick. Pour syrup to egg yolks in thin streams while beating. Cool. Cream butter. Blend in egg yolk mixture and rum. Fill and cover wafers with filling. Sprinkle top with chopped cashew nuts. Serve chilled.

TOCINO DEL CIELO

¼ k. sugar	6 egg yolks
2 c. water	1 whole egg

Boil water and sugar in a saucepan, until syrupy. Use ¼ cup syrup to line molds. Set remaining syrup aside. Beat egg yolks and whole egg until blended. Stir in the rest of the syrup. Strain mixture. Spoon in mold. Cook tocinos in bain marie for 10 minutes. Bake for 10 minutes or until set. Cool, unmold on small paper cups.

SUSPIROS DE PILI

¾ c. Liberty Condensada	¼ c. white sugar
1 c. chopped pili	1 tbsp. water
2 egg yolks	1 egg white
1 tbsp. butter	Margarine for greasing

Paper cups

Combine Liberty Condensada, pili and eggyolks in a skillet, and cook stirring constantly over low heat. When thick, add the butter and blend well. Grease paper cups with margarine and fill with the pili mixture. Set aside. Combine sugar and water in a saucepan. Cook until syrup forms a soft ball when dropped in cold water. Beat egg whites and when stiff, add the syrup little by little, beating constantly. Top each filled cup with meringue. Bake in a moderate oven (350°F.) 15 minutes or until meringue is slightly browned. 1 cup grated macapuno may be used instead of pili nuts.

From the Liberty Milk Cookbook.

185

GINATAAN

1 coconut, grated
1 tbsp. sago or tapioca
½ k. gabi, diced
½ k. ubi, diced
½ k. camote, diced

4 saba bananas, sliced
crosswise
6 sections nangka or bread
fruit, in strips
1 c. sugar

Add ½ cup warm water to coconut. Put in a cheesecloth, wring to get 1 cup thick coconut milk. Strain and set aside. Repeat using 2 cups warm water. Strain and boil. Add tapioca, gabi and ubi. Cook until half done. Drop camote, bananas and nangka. Blend in sugar. Pour thick coconut milk before removing. Cook until done. Stir occasionally.

MAJA BLANCA

2 coconuts, grated
2 c. warm water

½ c. cornstarch
½ c. sugar
½ c. water

Place grated coconuts in a cheese cloth. Wring to get 1 cup thick coconut milk. Strain and set aside. Repeat using 2 cups warm water. Strain and set aside. Boil thick coconut milk until oil comes out and "latik" is brown but not burnt. Set aside. Blend cornstarch and sugar thoroughly in a bowl. Add the water. Set aside. Boil thin coconut milk, stirring constantly. Add sugar-cornstarch mixture and stir to prevent lumps. Cook to boiling, stir for 3 minutes or until a cooked flavor is obtained. Grease a 13" rectangular pan with coconut oil. Spoon maja, allow to set. Slice in squares or diamond shapes. Arrange in a platter or saucers. Serve with latik.

ROYAL BIBINGKA

3 eggs

¾ c. granulated sugar

2 c. all-purpose flour

4 tsps. baking powder

1¼ c. coconut milk

½ c. grated cheese

Banana leaves, wilted

Beat eggs until light and creamy. Add sugar gradually beating well after each addition. Sift flour and baking powder together. Beat dry ingredients alternately with coconut milk. Pour batter into 2 9" layer cake pans that have been greased and lined with wilted banana leaves. Bake at 350°F. 10 minutes. Take out pans and sprinkle with cheese. Bake 20 minutes more. Brush twice with margarine while baking. When done, brush again with margarine and sprinkle with sugar. Serve with freshly grated coconut.

Pies 'N' Pastries

APPLE PIE
Crust:

Prepare pastry for 2-crust pie.*   Prepare the filling.

Filling

¼ c. brown sugar, packed
¼ c. granulated sugar
2 tbsps. all-purpose flour
¼ tsp. salt
¾ tsp. cinnamon

¼ tsp. nutmeg
2 tbsps. butter or margarine
1½ c. sliced canned apples or
8 - 10 green tart apples,
    sliced

Combine first 7 ingredients together.   Blend well.   Coat apples gently
with sugar-spice mixture.   Spoon into pie crust.   Cover with crust.
Bake at 425°F. about 40-45 minutes or until apples are cooked and pie
crust is golden brown.

* Recipe of pastry for 2-crust pie, on page 201.

ENSAIMADA ESPECIAL

First Beating:

2 tsps. yeast
½ tsp. sugar
¾ c. lukewarm water

1 c. bread flour
½ c. lukewarm Carnation
Evaporated Milk

Measure into bowl ¾ c. lukewarm water. Sprinkle yeast over water. Stir until dissolved. Stir in lukewarm Carnation Evaporated Milk, sugar and flour. Mix with wooden spoon until smooth. Cover the bowl with a clean towel (if preferred use a large pan or plate). Set the bowl into a pan of warm water until the mixture doubles in size (about 20 to 25 minutes).

Second Beating:

5 egg yolks (plus 1 egg
white), beaten

2 c. bread flour
¼ c. sugar

Mix the beaten yolks, sugar and flour. Beat well. Add to the above mixture. Knead and shape into a ball. Cover and let rise again in a pan of warm water until double in bulk (30 to 40 minutes).

Third Beating:

5 egg yolks (plus 1 egg
white), beaten
¾ c. creamed butter

2 c. bread flour
½ c. sugar
2 c. grated queso de bola

When above dough is double in volume, add beaten egg yolks and white sugar, flour and creamed butter. Mix. Place in a greased board. Knead until satiny and smooth (about 10 minutes). Shape into smooth ball. Place ball of dough into greased bowl. Cover and let rise until double in size (40 to 60 minutes). Punch down. Divide the dough into separate pieces. Roll each piece thinly on a greased board. Spread butter and sprinkle grated cheese on rolled out dough. Starting from one end, twist to form a cone. Grease molds and put in the twisted dough. Cover and let rise in a pan of warm water until dough has doubled (about 40 to 60 minutes. Remove from baking molds and let cool for 5 minutes. Top with creamed butter, sugar, and grated cheese (if preferred sprinkle with more sugar).

APPLE STREUSEL PIE
Crust

Prepare pastry for 1-crust 9" pie.*   Set aside.   Prepare filling.

Filling:

2½ c. fresh apples or 1 can
   apples, sliced
½ c. sugar
¼ c. brown sugar (firmly
   packed)

½ tsp. salt
¼ tsp. nutmeg
¾ tsp. cinnamon
2 tbsps. flour

Mix together all dry ingredients.   Toss lightly over every layer of apples.   Arrange into unbaked pie shell.   Set aside.   Prepare topping.

Topping

½ c. sifted flour
⅓ c. granulated sugar
2 tbsps. butter

1 c. coarsely grated cheddar
cheese
2 tbsps. Carnation Evaporated Milk

Combine flour and sugar. Cut in butter and cheese. Moisten with Carnation Evaporated Milk. Spread to cover pie. Bake at 350° F. 30-40 minutes or until brown.

BUCO PIE
Crust

Follow recipe for 2-8" crust pie.**   Prepare filling.

Filling

2 c. young coconut meat
   (buco), in slivers

¾ c. sugar
½ c. coconut water

½ c. Carnation
   evaporated milk
⅓ c. cornstarch

Blend ingredients together.   Cook stirring continuously until thick. Pour in pastry lined pan.   Top with second crust.   Bake at 400°F. until brown.   Serve cold.

Recipe of pastry for 1-crust pie, on page 204.
**Recipe of pastry for 2-crust pie, on page 201.*

SILVANAS

½ c. egg whites
1 c. granulated sugar
  *Butter Icing
¼ c. all purpose flour

½ c. cashew nuts, pounded
  until powdered and then
  sifted
1 c. cake crumb

Beat the egg whites until stiff. Add the sugar gradually. Fold in the flour and the cashew nuts. On a greased and floured cookie sheet, press the mixture through brown paper cone in shape of an oval. Bake in a pre-heated oven 200° F. for 15 minutes or until lightly brown. Let cool. Spread icing* on one cookie and cover with another. Spread a little icing on all sides and roll in cake crumbs.

BROWNIES

1½ c. butter or margarine
  2 c. sugar
  5 eggs
2½ c. all purpose flour
  ¾ c. cocoa

1 tsp. vanilla
1 tsp. salt
1½ c. chopped cashew nuts or
  walnuts

Cream butter and add sugar. Cream thoroughly. Add the eggs one at a time. Combine the dry ingredients. Add to the butter mixture and beat until blended. Stir in chopped nuts. Pour into a greased square or rectangular pan (a 13″ x 16″ serving tray may be used). Bake for 25 minutes at 350°F. or until done. Cut in diamond shapes and serve.

BANANA CREAM PIE

Prepare pastry for an 8″ pie.*   Prick pastry all over with fork and bake at 400°F. until golden brown.   Set aside.   Prepare filling.

Banana Cream Filling

¼ c. sugar	2 egg yolks, slightly beaten
3 tbsps. cornstarch	1 tbsp. butter
1½ c. Carnation Evaporated Milk scalded	½ tsp. vanilla
	2 ripe bananas (lacatꝺn)**

Combine sugar and cornstarch. Gradually stir in Carnation Evaporated Milk. Cook over double boiler stirring constantly until mixture thickens. Remove from heat. Gradually stir half of the mixture into the egg yolks. Pour back in saucepan and blend. Cook until mixture coats spoon. Blend in butter and vanilla. Cool. Prepare meringue.*** Arrange layers of sliced bananas on pie shell and cover with cream filling. Pile meringue and bake at 400°F. 8-10 minutes or until brown. Chill and serve.

Recipe of pastry for 1-crust pie, on page 204.
** 4 ripe firm mangoes may be substituted for bananas.
*** Recipe of meringue, on page 196.

CUSTARD SNOW PIE
Crust

Make pastry for 1-crust 8″ pie.*   Prick all over with a fork and bake at 400°F. for 45 minutes or until brown.   Prepare custard.

Custard

¼ cup all-purpose flour	3 egg yolks
½ tsp. salt	1½ c. Carnation Evaporated Milk
¾ c. sugar	1 tsp. vanilla
1 egg	

Sift flour, salt and sugar together. Break in egg and egg yolks, blend. Stir in Carnation Evaporated Milk, beat until smooth. Cook over double boiler until thick. Add vanilla. Cool and pour on baked pastry shell. Set aside. Prepare meringue.** Swirl or pull up points for decorative top. Bake at 400°F. for 8-10 minutes. Cool gradually in a place where there is no draft.

Recipe of pastry for 1-crust pie, on page 204.
** Recipe of meringue, on page 196.

AU BON VIVANT ORANGE TART

Creme Patissiere:

1½ c. Carnation Evaporated Milk	¼ c. sugar
1 c. water	¼ c. flour
5 pcs. eggs, whole	¼ tsp. vanilla
	2-3 tbsps. Cointreau

Scald Carnation Evaporated Milk and water. Mix flour, sugar and eggs together. Pour in scalded milk and blend thoroughly. Cook to make medium thick cream. Cool and add Cointreau and set aside.

Crust:

2 c. all purpose flour	½ c. sugar
1 egg, whole	¼ c. butter or margarine

Mix all the ingredients for the crust together. Knead and form into a ball. Roll out and place into an 8" pie plate. Bake crust. Cool. Pour cream on pie crust about ¾" thick.

Topping:

6-7 Fresh oranges, sliced across, thinly.
½ c. sugar

Arrange orange slices in circular form. Sprinkle with sugar. Bake for 10 to 15 minutes or until done. Brush top with syrup.

BUTTERSCOTCH PIE

Make pastry for 1-crust pie.*   Prick all over with a fork and bake at 400°F. until golden brown.   Prepare filling.

Filling

¼ c. brown sugar	¼ c. all-purpose flour
¼ c. water	1½ c. Carnation Evaporated Milk
⅓ c. brown sugar	3 egg yolks, beaten
¼ c. butter	Meringue**

Caramelize the brown sugar. Pour water all at once, boil until caramelized sugar is melted. Set aside. Combine sugar and flour. Blend caramelized sugar and Carnation Evaporated Milk. Cook over double boiler stirring continuously until thick. Remove from fire. Stir 1/4 of hot mixture into eggyolks. Pour back to pan and continue cooking until mixture coats the spoon. Blend in butter and pour into baked pie shell. Set aside. Prepare meringue for an 8" pie crust. Spread meringue evenly over cooled pie filling and brown at 350° F. for 15-20- minutes.

* Recipe of pastry for 1-crust pie, on page 204.
** Recipe for meringue, page 196.

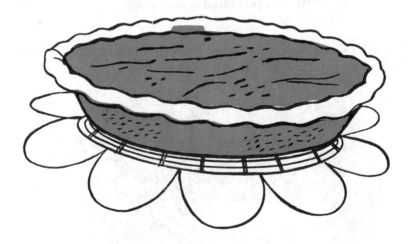

LENGUAS DE GATO

½ c. butter
½ c. sugar
3 egg whites

1 c. flour
Pinch of salt
¼ tsp. vanilla

Preheat oven to 400°F. Grease and flour baking sheets. Cream butter and sugar together. Beat in unbeaten egg whites, a little at a time, beating well after each addition. Lastly, fold in flour, salt and vanilla. Fill pastry bag or cookie press using the smallest plain tips. Press out thin strips of batter about 2″ long. Leave 2″ space between cookies for spreading. Bake about 7 minutes or until edges of cookies are golden brown (center should remain light). Remove cookies from baking sheet at once. If allowed to cool cookies will stick to pan. Allow to cool and serve or store. To maintain crispness, store in dry sealed container.

SCOTCH SHORTBREAD

½ c. powdered sugar
1 c. butter
1 tsp. vanilla

2 c. flour
¼ tsp. salt
¼ tsp. baking powder

Sift powdered sugar. Cream butter. Add the sugar gradually until blended. Add 1 tsp. vanilla. Combine, then work in 2 cups flour, salt and baking powder with the hands. Roll out dough to thickness of ⅓-inch; or roll it between pieces of waxed paper. Cut into squares. Bake in a greased pan at 375°F. for about 20 minutes.

SPRITZ COOKIES

1 c. soft butter or margarine
⅔ c. sugar

3 egg yolks
1 tsp. vanilla

1½ c. all purpose flour

Mix thoroughly soft butter, sugar, egg yolks and vanilla. Work in flour with hands. Force the dough through cooky press onto ungreased baking sheet in letter S, rosettes, fluted bars or other desired shapes. Bake until set, but not brown. (About 7 to 10 minutes at 400°F.).

GRAHAM CRACKER CHOCOLATE PIE
Crust

1 8 inch pie plate	1 c. graham cracker crumbs
¼ c. butter, melted	¼ c. sugar

Combine crumbs, sugar and melted butter together.   Press to fit pie plate snugly.   Bake at 350°F. 20 minutes.   Prepare Filling.

Filling

¾-1 c. sugar	⅛ tsp. salt
⅓ c. flour	2 c. Carnation Evaporated Milk
⅓ c. cocoa	2 egg yolks
	1 tsp. vanilla

Combine sugar, flour, cocoa and salt in a saucepan. Stir in Carnation Evaporated Milk. Cook over double boiler until mixture thickens, stirring constantly. Remove from heat. Add ½ cup hot mixture to egg-yolks, pour back in saucepan and blend. Cook 5 minutes longer. Cool and add vanilla. Pour into baked crust. Set aside. Prepare Meringue. Bake in 350° F. oven till meringue is golden brown.

PIE MERINGUE
For 9″ Pie

3 egg whites	⅓ c. sugar
¼ tsp. cream of tartar	½ tsp. flavoring (if desired)

For 8″ Pie

2 egg whites	¼ c. sugar
¼ tsp. cream of tartar*	¼ tsp. flavoring (if desired)

Beat egg whites with cream of tartar until frothy.   Gradually beat in sugar, a little at a time.   Continue beating until stiff and glossy.   Beat in flavoring.   Pile meringue onto pie filling, being careful to seal the meringue onto edge of crust to prevent shrinking and weeping.   Swirl or pull up points for decorative top.   To cut meringue pie neatly, dip sharp knife into water, either warm or cold, shake off any excess drops, cut.   Repeat.

* 1 tsp. lemon juice may be substituted for cream of tartar in meringue.

BOAT TARTS

2 c. all-purpose flour
1 tsp. salt
2 tbsps. sugar
2 egg yolks

½ c. margarine or butter
2 tbsps. water
1 boat tart cutter
24 boat tart molds

Sift flour, salt and sugar into a bowl. Add the margarine and cut with a pastry blender until margarine is broken into fine particles. Sprinkle water, stir and gather mixture to form a dough. Chill. Roll out about ¼" thick. Cut with cutter and fit into boat tart shells. Fill with Cashew Nut Filling. Bake at 350°F. for 10 minutes or until brown.

Cashew Nut Filling

2 egg yolks
¾ c. sugar
¾ c. cashew nuts, chopped

⅓ c. margarine, melted
2 tbsps. Carnation Evaporated Milk
1 egg white

Beat egg yolks until lemon colored. Add sugar, cashew nuts, margarine and Carnation Evaporated Milk. Set aside. Beat egg white. Fold into cashew nuts mixture.

CARAMEL TARTS

Crust:

2 c. all purpose flour	1 c. butter or margarine
1 tsp. salt	2 egg yolks
2 tbsps. sugar	About 2 tbsps. water

Sift into a bowl the flour, salt and sugar. Add egg yolks and butter. Mix by hand until the butter is broken into fine particles. Add just enough water to hold mixture together. Chill thoroughly and roll out about ¼ inch thick. Shape and fit into boat containers. Bake in hot oven for about 15 minutes. Fill with caramel and top with merengue.

Filling:

1¼ c. brown sugar	3 egg yolks
⅓ c. water	¾ c. Carnation Evaporated Milk
½ c. butter or margarine	

Caramelize brown sugar. Add the flour, butter and Carnation Evaporated Milk. Cook over slow fire until thick. Add the beaten egg yolks off the fire. Cook for 5 minutes over a slow fire. Cool and fill tart shells. Top with meringue and bake in a slow oven until firm.

Meringue:

3 egg whites	A pinch of salt
¼ tsp. cream of tartar	6 tbsps. sugar

Beat the egg whites until stiff but not dry with a pinch of salt and cream of tartar. Gradually add the sugar, beating constantly. Top the tarts with the meringue using a cake decorator to make them attractive.

PINIPIG COOKIES

1 c. butter or margarine	2¼ c. all purpose flour
1½ c. sugar	2 tsps. baking powder
3 to 4 pcs. eggs, beaten	½ tsp. salt
½ tsp. dayap or lemon	3 c. pinipig, puffed*

Preheat oven to 350°F. Grease the cookie sheets. Cream shortening (butter or margarine) and sugar. Add beaten eggs, one at a time. Add flavoring. Combine flour, baking powder and salt. Add the dry ingredients to the creamed mixture and mix thoroughly. Lastly fold in puffed pinipig. Drop by teaspoonfuls onto the cookie sheets. Flatten with back of the tines of the fork. Bake in a moderate over for 15 minutes. Cool on wire rack.

* Deep fat fry pinipig to puff.

PILI-NUT PIE
Crust

Prepare pastry for one-crust 8″ pie.   Prepare filling.

Filling

2 tbsps. flour	¼ c. melted butter
¼ c. sugar	2 eggs
1 tsp. salt	½ c. Carnation Evaporated Milk
½ c. corn syrup	1 c. pili nuts, broken
¾ tsp. vanilla	

Combine flour, sugar and salt. Mix in syrup and melted butter. Beat in eggs with a fork and blend very well. Add Carnation Evaporated Milk, pili nuts and vanilla. Pour into an 8" pastry-lined pie pan. Bake at 375°F. for 50 minutes. Cool before serving.

From the Liberty Milk Cookbook.

LEMON CHEESE PIE
Crust

1¼ c. graham crackers   2 tbsps. sugar   ¼ c. butter, melted

Crush graham crackers then sift.   Measure into a bowl, add the sugar and blend well.   Stir in melted butter.   Press mixture firmly and evenly against bottom and sides of pie pan.   Set aside.   Prepare filling.

Filling

2-8 oz. cream cheese	2 tbsps. flour
2 tbsps. butter	⅓ c. Carnation Evaporated Milk
¾ c. sugar	¼ c. lemon juice
1 egg	grated rind of 1 lemon

Cream cheese and butter. Blend 'in flour and sugar and egg. Stir in Carnation Evaporated milk. Stir in lemon juice and rind. Pour into prepared pie shell. Sprinkle top with cracker crumbs. Bake at 350°F. for 25 minutes. Serve chilled.

* Recipe of pastry for 1-crust pie, on page 204.

MARSHMALLOW PIE

Prepare Stir-N-Roll Pastry for an 8" pie.* Prick all over with a fork and bake at 400°F. until brown. Set aside. Prepare filling.

Filling

24 large marshmallows
¼-⅓ c. fresh lemon juice
Grated rind of 1 lemon
5-6 drops yellow food coloring
if desired

1½ c. whipping cream, stiffly
beaten
Marshmallow for
garnishing

In saucepan heat marshmallow, lemon juice, rind and water, stirring constantly until marshmallows are melted. Add food coloring. Chill until mixture mounds slightly when dropped from a spoon. Fold in whipped cream. Pile in baked pie shell. Chill until set 2-3 hours. Garnish with marshmallow and broil until brown. Serve cold.

ORANGE MERINGUE PIE

Pie Shell

Follow recipe for 1-8" crust pie.** Prick all over with fork, bake at 400°F. for 45 minutes or until brown. Set aside. Prepare filling.

Orange Meringue Filling

3 tbsps. all-purpose flour
3 egg yolks
2 tbsps. lemon juice
¾ c. orange juice

½ tsp. grated orange rind
2 tbsps. water
⅓ c. sugar
3 egg whites

⅛ tsp. salt

Combine first 7 ingredients together. Blend and cook over double boiler until thick. Cool. Whip egg whites and salt until stiff but not dry. Fold into orange custard. Heap unto baked pie shell. Broil until brown.

* *Recipe of Stir-N-Roll Pastry, on page 204.*
** *Recipe of pastry for 1-crust pie, on page 204.*

STANDARD PASTRY FOR TWO-CRUST PIE

2 c. sifted all-purpose flour   ⅓ c. margarine
1 tsp. salt   3 tbsps. water
⅓ c. vegetable shortening

Measure flour into mixing bowl and mix salt through it. With pastry blender, cut in shortening until shortening particles are the size of peas. Sprinkle with water, a tbsp. at a time, mixing lightly with a fork until all the flour is moistened. Gather dough together with fingers until it cleans the bowl. Press firmly into a ball. Divide dough into 2 balls. Roll out larger dough between 2 strips of wax paper. Peel off top paper, place crust in pan, paper side up. Peel paper, fit pastry loosely into pan. Trim, leaving ½" over hanging edge. Set aside. Prepare filling. Pour into pastry-lined pan. Roll out remaining dough until large enough to extend 1" beyond edge of pie pan. Make several slits near center to allow steam to escape during baking. Carefully place pastry evenly on top of filling. Fold extra edge of top pastry under edge of lower pastry. Seal thoroughly by pressing together with fingers on edge of pie pan. Flute all around. Bake pie as directed in each recipe.

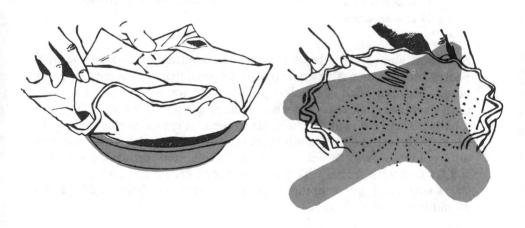

FRUIT TARTS

2¼ c. sifted all-purpose flour
¼ tsp. salt
½ c. shortening
¼ c. margarine

1 egg yolk, slightly beaten
5-6 tbsps. cold water
1 c. fruit cocktail, drained

Sift flour, and salt in a bowl.　Cut in shortening and margarine with pastry blender or with two knives until particles are the size of giant peas.　Moisten with egg yolk, sprinkle cold water a tbsp. at a time, until particles stick together when pressed gently.　Gather dough into a ball.　Cut into rounds 2½ in diameter.　Fit into molds and prick. Make 8-10 tart shells.　Chill ½ hour.　Bake at 450°F. 10-15 minutes until golden brown.　Cool.　Fill baked shells half full with cream filling,* cover with fruits.　Top with whipped cream or meringue.　For tarts with meringue topping:** return to oven and bake at 350°F. for 15 minutes or until brown.

* Recipe of cream filling, on page 203.
** Recipe of meringue, on page 196.

CREAM PUFFS

1 c. water	1 c. all-purpose flour
½ c. butter or margarine	4 eggs

Pre heat oven to 400°F. Heat water and butter to a rolling boil in saucepan. Add flour all at once and stir vigorously over low heat until mixture forms a ball. (about 1 min.) Remove from heat. Beat in eggs thoroughly, 1 at a time. Drop from a spoon onto ungreased baking sheet into mounds 3" apart. Bake 45-50 minutes or until puffed, golden brown and dry. Split cream puffs. Fill with cream filling. Dust with confectioners' sugar or dribble with caramelized sugar.

Cream Filling

½ c. sugar	2 c. Carnation Evaporated Milk
⅓ c. all-purpose flour	2 eggs, beaten
½ tsp. salt	1 tsp. vanilla

Mix sugar, flour and salt in saucepan. Blend in Carnation Evaporated Milk. Cock over medium heat, stirring until it boils. Boil 10 minutes. Remove from fire. Stir half of cream mixture into egg yolks. Pour back in saucepan and blend. Bring just to boil. Lower heat and cook stirring 10 minutes more or until mixture coats spoon. Cool, add vanilla and fill puffs.

EMPANADITAS

½ c. Carnation Evaporated Milk	1 egg yolk
½ tsp. calamansi or lemon	½ c. butter or margarine
juice or vinegar	2 c. all-purpose flour, sifted
Pinch of salt.	

Combine Carnation Evaporated Milk and acid. Let stand until milk is curdled. Cream margarine and egg yolk until light and fluffy. Sift flour and salt together. Stir alternately flour mixture and sour cream. Gather into a ball. Wrap in wax paper and chill for at least 1 hour. On a lightly floured board, roll out dough 1/8" thick and cut into 3" rounds. Put a teaspoon of filling on one half side of dough and fold in half moon shape. Dent edges with a fork. Bake empanaditas on a greased baking sheet at 350°F. 15-20 minutes or until brown.

Filling

1 c. chopped pili nuts	¼ c. sugar
¼ c. honey	2 tbsps. butter

Combine all ingredients in a saucepan and cook mixture until honey and sugar dissolve.

STANDARD PASTRY FOR ONE-CRUST PIE

1 ¼ c. all-purpose flour   ⅓ c. fat
½ tsp. salt   2 tbsps. margarine
2 tbsps. water

Sift flour and salt together into a bowl. Blend fat and margarine. Cut in with pastry blender until well blended. Sprinkle water over mixture and form into a ball, press firmly. Roll out dough between 2 pieces of wax paper. Peel off top paper. Place crust in pan, paper side-up. Peel paper, fit pastry loosely into pan. Trim, leaving ½" overhanging edge. Fold under and flute sides. Prick crust with fork. Set pie crust aside. Prepare filling.

STIR-N-ROLL PASTRY

1 ⅓ c. all-purpose flour, sifted   ⅓ c. cooking or salad oil
1 tsp. salt   3 tbsps. cold Carnation
Evaporated Milk

Mix flour and salt in a bowl. Pour into measuring cup the cooking oil and Carnation Evaporated Milk, but do not stir. Pour oil-milk mixture all at once into flour. Stir with fork, until mixed. Dough should look moist. but not sticky. Press into a smooth ball. Roll out gently to edges of wax paper. Dampen table top to prevent from slipping. Peel off top paper. Lift paper and pastry by top corners. Place paper-side-up in pie pan. Fit. Peel off paper. Flute all around. Set aside, and prepare filling.

TART AUX FRAISES
Strawberry Tart

Pastry

1½ c. all purpose flour   1 tbsp. sugar
⅓ c. butter   ⅓ c. water
¼ tsp. salt

Mix together. Knead and form into a ball. Roll out and place onto an 8″ pie plate. Bake until golden brown at 400°F. Prepare Cream Filling.

Cream Filling

2 c. scalded fresh milk   ⅓ c. sugar
6 tbsps. flour   4 egg yolks
3 drops vanilla

For Topping

1½ c. fresh strawberries   ¼ c. water   ½ c. apple or guava jelly

Scald milk. Mix flour, sugar and eggs together forming a paste. Add scalded milk. Cook to make a medium thick cream. Pour cream filling (½ full) on cooled pie crust and arrange strawberries on top. Dissolve ½ cup apple jelly with ¼ cup water over medium fire. Use to glaze pie.

PINEAPPLE-CALAMANSI PUNCH

2½ c. pineapple juice
½ c. calamansi juice
1 c. ice

6 tbsps. sugar
⅛ to ¼ c. light rum (depending
on desired strength of drink)

M ix all ingredients. Serve cold. Garnish with orange slices and maraschino cherries. Serves 5 to 6.
Note: Multiply to get desired number of servings.

PARTY PUNCH

6 c. pineapple juice
3 c. orange juice
1 c. lemon juice
1 c. water

1 c. sugar
24 whole cloves
4-3 inch sticks cinnamon
3 bottles ginger ale

½ c. light colored rum

Combine the juices. Boil water, sugar, spices together for five minutes. Cool and strain out spices. Add spiced syrup to juices. Chill thoroughly. At serving time, pour in ice-cold ginger ale and rum. Garnish with orange slices and maraschino cherries. Serves about 30 cups.

FRUIT PUNCH

2 c. boiling water
4 tsp. tea
¾ c. sugar
¾ c. orange juice

⅛ c. lemon juice
4 bottles ginger ale, cold
½ orange, sliced thin
Halved strawberries
(optional)

Pour fresh boiling water over tea; steep for 5 minutes. Strain. Add orange and lemon juices. Chill thoroughly. Add ginger ale and pour over ice in punch bowl. Float orange slices and halved strawberries.

Cocktails

BLOODY MARY

1 jigger Vodka	4 drops worcestershire sauce
3 oz. heavy tomato juice	dash salt
½ oz. fresh lemon juice	dash pepper

Shake well with cracked ice and serve.

FROZEN DAIQUIRI

Juice of ½ lime or lemon   1 jigger (1½ oz.) light rum

1 tsp. powdered sugar

Place 2 cups of shaved ice in a blender. Add ingredients and blend until consistency of snow. Serve immediately in champagne glass with straws.

GIMLET

1½ oz. Gin   ½ oz. Lime Juice Cordial

Slice of lemon and Cherry

Stir and serve in cocktail glass. Decorate with slice of lemon and cherry. Add ice if desired.

GIN AND TONIC

1 oz. Gin   **Quinine water**   **Piece of lemon**

Place St. George Dry Gin in a highball glass half-filled with cracked ice.
Squeeze piece of lemon into it.   Fill glass with quinine water and stir.

MARTINI

1 oz. Gin   **3 dashes Dry Vermouth**
An olive and lemon peel

Stir with cracked ice and strain into a chilled cocktail glass.   Add olive
and a twist of lemon peel.

TOM COLLINS

1 tbsp. sugar   **1½ jiggers of gin**
Juice of 1 lemon   **Club Soda**
slices of lemon and cherry

Fill tall glass with ice cubes.   Add sugar, juice of lemon and gin.   Fill
with club soda.   Stir.   Decorate with slices of lemon and cherry.

PINK LADY

¼ oz. Grenadine   **¾ oz. gin**   **White of 1 egg**

Shake grenadine and gin with egg white.   Strain into cocktail glass.

COURTESY: LA TONDEÑA, INC.

CALORIE CHART
OF COMMON FOODS

Food Item	Calories
1 tbsp. butter	100
1" cube cheddar cheese	113
½ c. evaporated milk	173
1 tbsp. cooking oil	124
1 tbsp. margarine	100
1 tbsp. mayonnaise	92
1 med. lakatan banana	55
1 med. bungulan banana	48
1 med. sized orange	70
1 med. apple	76
200 gm. papaya, ripe	92
1 tsp. calamansi juice	4
1 c. canned pineapple juice	121
½ c. cubed pineapple in syrup	114
½ c. canned peaches	87
1 c. shredded cabbage	25
½ c. beans (habichue-las)	17
½ c. Mongo beans (un-cooked)	323

Food Item	Calories
1 med. boiled potato	120
½ c. sitaw	14
½ c. Sweet Potato (ca-mote)	98
½ c. peanuts	406
100 gms. pork (with med. fat)	484
100 gms. beef (kabilu-gan)	221
100 gms. chicken	97
100 gms. bangus	121
100 gms. dalag	74
100 gms. hasa-hasa	95
100 gms. lapu-lapu	84
100 gms. shrimps	100
½ c. tuna	198
1 slice loaf bread	62
1 c. cooked rice	178
1 2" × 2" cracker	34
1 med. egg	64
1 tbsp. sugar	48
12 oz. bottle beer	162 - 200
8 oz. cola soft drink	110
1 c. milk	160 - 170

WEIGHTS AND MEASURES

1	teaspoon	— ⅓	tablespoon
1	tablespoon	— 3	teaspoons
2	tablespoons	— ⅛	cup (1 ounce)
4	tablespoons	— ¼	cup
5-⅓	tablespoons	— ⅓	cup
8	tablespoons	— ½	cup
16	tablespoons	— 1	cup
⅜	cup	— 5	tablespoons
⅝	cup	— 10	tablespoons
1	cup	— ½	pint
2	cups	— 1	pint
2	pints	— 1	quart
4	quarts	— 1	gallon
8	quarts	— 1	peck
4	pecks	— 1	bushel
1	pound	— 16	ounces
1	fluid ounce	— 2	tablespoons
16	fluid ounces	— 1	pint
1	jigger	— 1-½	fluid ounces (3 tablespoons)

APPROXIMATE CAN SIZES

Can Size	Weight	Contents
6 ounces	6 ounces	¾ cup
8 ounces	8 ounces	1 cup
No. 1	11 ounces	1-⅓ cups
12 ounces	12 ounces	1-½ cups
No. 303	16 ounces	2 cups
No. 2	20 ounces	2-½ cups
No. 2-½	28 ounces	3-½ cups

GLOSSARY

Chinese Ingredients

Ang-Chow — sediment or "latak" from glutinous rice wine.
Chaysim — pechay with flowers
Chorizo canton — Chinese sausage
Kangiodro
Misi — salted yellow-brown soybean
Misu — soy bean paste
Oyster Sauce — cantonese sauce made of ground dried oysters and salt.
Ngo-yong — all spice powder, several kinds of spices.
Tofu — soybean cheese, soft
Tahure — salted soybean cheese. There are two varieties, red and white.
Tawpe — dried soybean milk skin
Tausi — fermented soybean curd
Tokwa — soybean cheese, hard
Toyo — black, salty sauce from soyabeans; soy sauce
Aji-no-moto — a brand of monosodium glutamate
Tahu — geerlig cheese

Beef

Bias — shank
Kabilugan — flank
Kadera — rib roast
Kalitiran — beef shoulder (boneless)
Librilyo — omassum (stomach)
Paypay — chuck
Pierna corta at pierna larga — Round Cut
Punta y pecho — brisket
Solomilyo — tenderloin
Tadyang — plate
Tagiliran, hulihan — sirloin steak
Tagiliran, gitna — porterhouse steak
Tapadera — cow's rump
Ulo — head
Utak — brain

Fish and Shellfish

Abalone — sea ear
Alimasag — crabfish
Alimango — crab
Apahap — sea bass
Bagoong-alamang — small shrimps, salted and fermented
Bakokong moro — fresh water porgy
Balatan — trepang
Bangus — milkfish
Bidbid — ten pounder
Bitchu-bitchu — shrimp fritter
Dalag — mudfish
Dapa — rough scaled brill
Dilis — long jawed anchovy
Halaan — clams
Lapu-lapu — spotted grouper
Maya-maya — malabar red snapper
Shrimp juice — to obtain: pound the heads of shrimps, add water and strain.
Sugpo — tiger prawn
Tahong — salt water mussel
Talaba — oyster
Talangka — small crabs
Tinapa — smoked fish

Noodles

Bihon — rice noodles
Mike — wheat noodles
Miswa — fine wheat noodles
Pancit Canton — dried chinese noodles
Sotanghon — mung bean starch noodle

Pork

Goto — tripe
Lapay — pork spleen
Likod — pork back fat
Liempo sa tiyan — pork plate fat
Liempo sa hulihan — porkloin chop
Lomo — tenderloin

Pata — pig's feet
Paypay — pork shoulder (Boston butt)
Pigi — fresh pork ham
Sitsaron — pork cracklings
Tadyang — pork spareribs

Poultry

Kalapati pitson — squab
Balun-balunan — gizzard
Itlog ng pugo — quail eggs

Vegetables

Abitsuwelas — snap beans or green beans
Ampalaya — bittermelon
Achara — pickled vegetables
Apulid — water chestnuts
Batao — hyacinth bean
Dilaw — turmeric
Gabi — taro roots
Garbanzos — chickpea
Labong — bamboo shoot
Labanos — radish
Langka — jackfruit
Letsugas — native lettuce
Mongo — mung bean
Mustasa — mustard plant
Niyog, buko — coconut, young
Patola — sponge gourd
Pechay or petsay — Chinese cabbage
Pechay with flowers — chaysim
Remolatsa — beets
Bulaklak ng saging, tuyo — dried banana
    flowers
Saging, puso — banana heart
Sibuyas tagalog — native onions or shallots
Sinkamas — yam bean
Sitaw — yard-long bean
Sitsaro — or chicharo; sweet pea
Toge — mung bean sprout
Ubi — yam
Ubod — heart of palm

Upo — bottle gourd
Wansuey — coriander
Sigadillas — winged bean

Miscellaneous

Atsuete seeds — anatto seeds
Atsuete water-to obtain: soak ½ cup at-
    suete in 1 cup warm water, strain.
Bay leaf — the aromatic leaf of the bay
    tree, dried and used as seasoning.
Calamansi — native lemon
Capers — the flower buds of the caper bush,
    pickled and used for flavoring sauces.
Chorizo de bilbao — Spanish sausage
Croutons — bread fried in butter, olive oil
    or any kind of oil or toasted in oven
    until crisp.
Condensada — sweetened condensed milk
Dayap — lime
Dilaw juice or turmeric juice — to obtain:
    pound dilaw or turmeric acid water and
    extract juice.
Ginger juice — pound ginger root, add wa-
    ter and extract juice.
Linga — sesame seeds
Morcillas — blood sausage
Nido — bird's nest
Oregano — any of a number of plants of
    the mint family especially Origanum
    Bulgare, the fragrant leaves of which
    are used in seasoning.
Patis — concentrated juice of salted fish,
    fish sauce.
Rice water — water obtained from washing
    uncooked rice.
Rice wine — wine obtained from glutinous
    rice.
Rock salt — coarse salt
Sago — tapioca
Salitre — commonly known as saltpeter;
    chem. name — potassium nitrate.
Taingang-daga — black wood ear

ABOUT THE AUTHORS

NORA DAZA

An alumna of the University of the Philippines, where she earned her B.S. in Home Economics, she added a Master of Science (major Restaurant and Institution Management) from Cornell University in Ithaca, New York. It was Cornell that awarded her membership in the Phi Kappa Phi Honor Society.

She has held the position of vice-president of the Philippine Association of Nutrition, Secretary of the Hotel and Restaurant Association of the Philippines; Adviser-Admiral Homemakers Club; Director, Hotel and Tourist Industries of the Philippines and President, Philippines Economists in Business.

Nora Daza pioneered in giving formal cooking lessons at Manila. She is the proud owner of Au Bon Vivant Ermita and Makati and Aux Iles Philippines in Paris. Now, the Maharlika Restaurant at the Philippine Center, 556 Fifth Avenue, New York City (bet 45th & 46th St.).

MARILES DAZA

The daughter of Nora Daza taking Hotel and Restaurant Administration at the University of the Phil. with the hope of improving the family's business. In the summer of 1973, she tested all the recipes published in this book. This experience gave her a further insight on Philippine cooking.

Added to her culinary abilities, Mariles also worked as Assistant Manager of Aux Iles Philippines, Paris and is presently enrolled at Sorbonne University.